The Champagne Spy

WOLFGANG LOTZ

The
Champagne Spy

ISRAEL'S MAN
IN EGYPT

VALLENTINE MITCHELL
LONDON • CHICAGO

First published in 1972 by VALLENTINE MITCHELL
Paper edition in 2022

Catalyst House, 720 Centennial Court, Centennial Park
Elstree, WD6 3SY, UK

814 N. Franklin Street
Chicago, IL 60610, USA

www.vmbooks.com

British Library Cataloguing in Publication Data
an entry can be found on request

ISBN 978 0 85303 653 1 (paper)
ISBN 978 1 80371 000 6 (ebook)
ISBN 978 1 80371 006 8 (kindle)

Acknowledgements
To Wolfgang Lotz and Stern Magazine; *The Jewish Observer*;
Israel Press and Photographic Agency for use of their photos in this book.

Library of Congress Cataloging-in-Publication Data
an entry can be found on request

To Waltraud

Contents

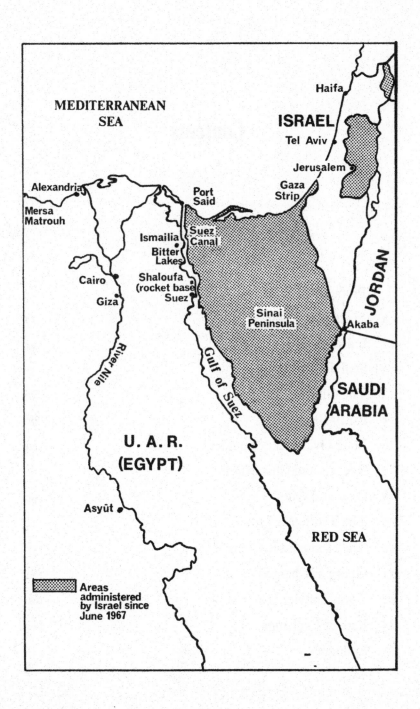

Preface

This is the true story of my life as an Israeli secret agent in Egypt. Unlike many exaggerated and tendentious accounts of my work that found their way into the world's press and the world's media, this is the only factual account. Of course certain details still come under the heading 'Classified Material', and cannot therefore be included; but apart from changing a very few names in order to protect friends and innocent people whom I wish no harm, the facts concerning my activities and experiences have in no way been altered. In some cases actual transcripts of court records have been used to amplify certain events, and newspaper accounts, letters and documents have also been included to clarify details of my operations.

I would like to take this opportunity to thank my publishers, and particularly Anthony Masters and Jeremy Robson, for their ready co-operation in preparing this book for the press.

WOLFGANG LOTZ
Tel-Aviv 1972

I

Making of a Spy

'Herr Lotz. This Court has found you guilty as charged. You have been found guilty of continued and repeated acts of espionage and sabotage on behalf of Israel and directed against the United Arab Republic...The penalty for the crimes you have committed is death...Frau Lotz. This Court has found you...'

I woke in a sweat and jumped from my bed. The sun was already streaming through the shutters and from the distance I could hear cars threading their noisy way towards Tel-Aviv. It must have been later than I imagined for Waltraud was already on the terrace, sipping coffee and reading the morning paper. She pointed to the headline – 'Wedding of the Spies' – and the photo beneath. There I stood, dressed in a dark suit and holding one of the poles of the bridal canopy, Prime Minister Golda Meir beside me, and the bride she had just given away, Marcelle Ninio, smiling happily. It all seemed a long way from Cairo, our arrest, and those other newspaper headlines blazing for weeks on end the theatrical details of our public trial.

At our trial, which began on July 27, 1965, and lasted

for nearly a month, I claimed German nationality – and further claimed that, as a German, I had been approached by the Israeli Secret Service and asked to spy for them in Egypt. I also claimed to have accepted – and suggested that my reasons for doing so were purely financial. In fact I considered my cover almost foolproof, for although I had left Germany in 1933 to settle in Israel, and was an Israeli citizen, I had retained dual nationality – and so my German papers were absolutely genuine.

I was born in Mannheim in 1921. My father, Hans, was a theatre director in Berlin and was later appointed director of the Hamburg State Theatre. My mother, Helene, was a Jewish actress. I inherited a certain degree of acting ability from them both – a vital asset to my profession in Egypt. I developed a sort of bombastic charm, was an excellent raconteur and a good mimic. I played the part of a wealthy, charming and generous man with good connections and a ready sense of humour.

Because my parents were not religious and because my father was a Gentile I was not circumcised – a factor that was to prove vital in substantiating my cover story and saving my life. I grew up in Berlin and from 1931 attended the Mommsen Gymnasium. Shortly after I joined the Gymnasium my parents divorced, and not long after the divorce my father died. In 1933 my mother emigrated to Palestine, taking me with her. She was a Jewess, the Nazis had just come into power and she knew that there was no future for her – or me – in Germany. When we arrived in Palestine my mother, after a struggle, found work as an actress in the Habimah Theatre. Like so many other immigrants from Europe she found life in Palestine desperately hard. She was used to the vivacious, sophisticated Berlin life and had found instead a comparative wilderness – an undeveloped country that demanded its immigrants be pioneers. She spoke no Hebrew, knew no one. I, at twelve, had less hardship than my mother. Shortly after arriving in Palestine I went to an agricultural school in Ben-Shemen where I grew to love horses – little realizing how important a role they were to play in my adult life.

As the years went by hostility began to intensify between the Arabs and the Jews. In 1937, when I was sixteen, I joined the Haganah, the Underground Army of the Jewish Community in Palestine. At the time Ben-Shemen was completely surrounded by Arab towns and villages and could be reached only in a heavily guarded armoured bus. Our duties included escorting that bus (and its illegal cargo of weapons) as well as guarding Ben-Shemen itself and the surrounding area, mostly on horseback.

When the Second World War broke out, I forged my birth date and joined the British Army as a volunteer, undergoing commando training. I now spoke Hebrew, Arabic, German and English – a great advantage to the British who quickly transferred me to Egypt. I spent the war in Egypt and North Africa and at the conclusion of hostilities emerged as a Quartermaster Sergeant. At the time I had a rust-red handlebar moustache which earned me the nickname of 'Rusty'. Gradually I was building up a series of abilities which needed a more demanding outlet than the Haifa Oil Refineries where I was given an administrative post after the war. I therefore joined in smuggling arms for the Haganah. My double life had begun.

This period of my life lasted for about three years – until 1948, when the first Arab-Israel war broke out. Immediately I joined up, was made a Lieutenant and placed in command of a company of half-trained immigrants. Our company took part in the violent skirmishes around that Latrun area – where we battled to establish the so-called Burma Road, south of Latrun, and unblock the route to Jerusalem. At the end of the war the independent state of Israel was a reality. Now, used to soldiering and unsure of what to do in civilian life, I stayed in the army as an officer in combat units and training command. I gained the rank of

major and during the Suez Campaign of 1956 was company
commander in an infantry brigade which captured the town
of Rafah, in the Negev.

But all the time age was creeping up on me, and my
military duties were becoming more and more routine and
administrative. I had, during the course of the last twenty
years, been married twice – and divorced twice; and it was
at this point, when life seemed to be growing dull, that I
was approached by the Israeli Secret Service. At the time I
was astonished, and after much heart-searching and before
making up my mind I decided to consult a close friend who
held a senior position in Israeli Intelligence. I wanted to
know whether he thought me suited for this kind of work.
'According to my experience,' he told me enigmatically, 'one
of two things will happen. Either you will return home
after a few weeks saying you can't stand the strain on your
nerves; or else, after a very short time, you will begin to
swim like a fish in water.'

And swim I did. Looking back now, I realize that my
choice as a potential spy was in fact no accident and showed
the Israeli Secret Service at its shrewdest. Although I was
only half-Jewish, I was nationalistic and was used to serving
my country. Because of my German background I could
easily be passed off as a German. I was blond, stocky and
thoroughly Teutonic in gesture, manner and looks. I was a
hard drinker and the very epitome of an ex-German officer.
These qualities, combined with my inherited acting ability,
made me a predictable enough choice. I would take orders,
I was unlikely to be easily scared, and I would certainly
not indulge in any dangerous introspection on my forthcoming predicament.

The training began. It was both intensive and exhausting,
but it had to it a strange and rather grim fascination, for
my proposed infiltration into Egypt was planned as a well-
administered military campaign. First of all it was necessary
to understand thoroughly the complicated ironies of the

Egyptian political situation – a situation that was to become all too clear after only a few weeks in Egypt. Yet at the time of my training I merely learned almost by heart the many details about Egypt which would enable me to discover the information the Israelis needed.

Gamal Abdul Nasser had come to power, by means of a bloodless coup d'état, on July 22, 1952. I remember being amazed at the ease with which the decadent Farouk monarchy was overthrown. The coup was well planned but not well carried out. Communications, for instance, were not cut off because the senior officer on duty was out seeing a film when the alert message came through to his home. Nasser was stopped and held up by the police on his way to supervise the coup because the tail-lights of his car were faulty, and later he was almost arrested by his own men. It was a tough, confused and chaotic night for everybody but the next morning the American Ambassador, Jefferson Caffery, was visited by Ali Sabri, one of Nasser's lieutenants, and quietly informed that a bloodless coup had taken place, that Farouk had been deposed, that Neguib had been elected President, that Nasser had been elected Prime Minister, and that the new regime wished to continue friendly relations with the United States.

On the surface all looked well. Despite the enormous gulf between the administration of Egypt and the people of Egypt, Neguib's presidency and Nasser's premiership had a good image. Everyone was tired of Farouk and the country's disastrous economic situation. The new rulers promised to stabilize the economy and to improve the conditions of the peasantry by introducing agrarian reform, and, sensibly, they made no controversial statements regarding Israel. The Americans therefore watched Egypt benevolently from the sidelines and allowed the new regime to find its feet. The last thing they wanted to initiate or to support was the kind of situation which existed in Syria – repetitive coups, interchangeable military juntas and openly unscrupul-

ous leaderships. Communist infiltration was active and Egypt
already possessed a fairly strong but politically unrepresented
Communist Party which, like the Moslem Brotherhood, was
predicting revolutionary movement and overthrows during
Farouk's time. Other Arab countries, despite both Russian
and American aid, were continually in a state of economic
turmoil and social uproar. The monarchs were decadent and
tottering but the revolutionaries were inept. A strong leader
in Egypt, the Americans thought, would stand out not only
as an example of stability to these unstable factions but would
also serve to cement the basis of a proper pro-Western
United Arab Republic.

There was no doubt that Nasser had inherited an extra-
ordinarily difficult situation. The material he had at his
disposal was hardly promising, and the people as a whole
completely lacking in any nationalistic spirit. The peasantry
and workers particularly were apathetic and indifferent, considering themselves second-class citizens. The deep-rooted
problem was corruption. Bribery was part of the Egyptian
way of life, and money changed hands so often that few were
scrupulous to avoid what was not so much a temptation
as an in-built custom. And it was this very weakness that the
Israeli Secret Service realized I could play on when I
arrived in Egypt.

At first the leaders of the Revolution were regarded as
saviours, for most of the aristocrats of Farouk's time were
greatly hated and feared. But although Nasser did make some
attempts to improve the lot of the people, repressive measures
were an integral part of his policy of nation building – and
obviously these were bitterly resented. The measures included wide-scale imprisonment without trial and political
persecution.

During the early years of his regime Nasser adopted a
'moderate' approach to the inflammatory issue of Israel, but
gradually his policy hardened, and a series of terrorist raids
from the Gaza Strip into Israeli territory brought matters

to the boil and resulted in the Suez Campaign of 1956 – a
disaster, from Egypt's point of view. Further troubles followed in Syria and Jordan up until February 1958 when a
union was forged between Syria and Egypt. Nasser was at
the height of his power, but in Cairo the prisons were burst-
ing with political prisoners, imprisoned either without a trial
or alternatively falling victims to elaborate show trials.
Conditions were appalling, arrests widespread. Nasser, the
man of the people, had become a despot.

The position of the Jews, in Egypt, meanwhile, worsened.
Here was another challenge – another reason for my taking
on the job. For centuries Jews had lived in Egypt peaceably
alongside the Arabs. There was no friction, no anti-Semitism.
The Jews were highly thought of by Arab businessmen
and were also known to be excellent employers: their em-
ployees were well looked after and cared for when they
were sick. Rather like the better Pashas, the Jews practised
a highly ethical feudal system which was much respected,
and many Jewish families continued to support their old
retainers from generations back. A large percentage of Jews
were goldsmiths, many were shopkeepers and some were
in the professions. This ethnic spread worked well, despite
the fact that, in common with their counterparts in Europe,
they were not allowed to rise above a certain grade in the
civil service. But even this restriction did not provoke an
anti-Semitic situation – it was simply an accepted fact and
was hardly thought about or questioned, except by the more
intellectual and liberal-thinking among the Jewish population.

In 1954, however, Nasser had decided to start an anti-
Semitic campaign. It took the shape of sequestration of
Jewish properties and personal possessions, and was done
primarily to fill the country's coffers. The ex-Nazis employed by Nasser were most anxious to strip away Jewish
influence in Egypt and were naturally highly voluble in

B

their support of his campaign. A plan was launched which was roughly shaped as follows: All Jewish money, property and assets were to be confiscated over a five-year period so as not to draw immediate attention to the situation. Jewish businesses were to be nationalized, and all Jews were to be dismissed from their jobs in both the civil service and private enterprise. Between 2,000 and 2,500 Jewish men were to be imprisoned and then released after a period of months. The system would then be put into operation again with the same numbers of different men. Luckily for the Jewish population the Egyptians were enjoying particularly good relations with the Americans at this period and so the persecution was less rigid and barbaric than it would have been had the Soviet Union and the exiled Nazis had greater influence.

Some 100,000 Jews were living in Egypt at this time, but (understandably) a large number of younger Jews left the country, emigrating to Israel or Europe as soon as these measures came into force. However, the older and richer Jews were loath to leave Egypt which they regarded as their homeland. For two years, despite the privations of Nasser's plan, this Jewish section continued to hang on. At the outbreak of war between Egypt and Israel in 1956 almost all the remaining Egyptian Jews were imprisoned while Jews of European origin were expelled and their property sequestered. In 1957, after suffering under incredibly squalid conditions and being perpetually beaten up and tortured, the majority of the Egyptian Jews were released and warned that unless they left the country their lives would be in considerable jeopardy.

As I trained and continued to digest masses of material concerning Egypt I learned also about the activities of some of those ex-Nazis Nasser had invited into Egypt – primarily to reorganize his army.

*   *   *

Having studied the Egyptian situation thoroughly I set about working out a convincing cover story. Ironically I found that it was necessary to become a German again and to achieve this I redesigned my past as follows: Rather than leaving Germany in 1933 I had remained at the Mommsen Gymnasium in Berlin. After my final examinations there I had joined the 115th Division of Rommel's Afrika Korps, where I stayed for the duration of the Second World War.* After the war I spent eleven years in Australia where I made my fortune as a race-horse owner and also bred horses. Then homesickness sent me back to Germany – the supposed homeland that I was to leave a year later for Cairo.

On this basis I was to be sent to Germany where I would register myself in Berlin, pointing out to the authorities there that I had had enough of Israel and wanted to become a German citizen again. My superiors and I fully realized that my cover, like any cover, had its weaknesses and the danger here lay in the possibility of someone checking back far enough in the German records office to discover the truth. The alternative was to work with false papers, but after weighing up the pros and cons we decided that the advantage of genuine papers far outweighed the risks involved. This resulted in my being one of the few secret agents ever to have worked under his real name, with his own genuine papers.

In an attempt to confuse any subsequent later investigations I was to move from address to address. In fact I was to spend twelve months in the country – simply making myself at home and refamiliarizing myself with the then contemporary German scene.

Finally, before I left for Germany, I learned the most valuable lesson I was ever to learn – the details behind the structure of Egypt's Intelligence Service and also the realities

---

* The story in fact suited me perfectly because during my service with the British army in Egypt I had taken part in the interrogation of P.O.W.'s from that very corps: so I knew many details – units, names of officers, etc. – which would substantiate my story if necessary.

of spying in Egypt. In fact spying activities had already
reached absurd proportions at the very beginning of Nasser's
regime, and from then on the escalation was incredible.
The whole intelligence set-up was increased and blown-up
to incredible proportions. Generally speaking the military
intelligence dealt mainly with ground and air reconnaissance
of purely military objectives. The Egyptian intelligence
machine consisted of two major departments, each of
which was sub-divided into a number of branches and
sections. By far the most important of these departments
was the so-called Muhabbarat El-Amma, or General Intelligence Agency (GIA). The other, Mabahes El-Amma, was the
Secret Police. The GIA was responsible to the President
personally and had almost unlimited powers. It could
and did kill, torture, terrorize, and confiscate property at
will and without any official authorization. Its general
duties were not clearly defined. It carried out espionage
and counterespionage activities as well as, in many cases,
actual police work. The secret police, on the other hand,
came directly under the Minister of Interior and dealt with
internal security, political security, and only in rare cases
with actual criminal investigation which was usually left
to the uniformed police.

There existed a great deal of professional jealousy and
competition between these two departments to the extent
that they frequently refused to co-operate with each other
and exchange information. Often they actually sabotaged
each other's work.

At the disposal of each of the two agencies was any
number of unpaid spies and informers. Practically every servant, doorman, taxi-driver, shopkeeper, hotel employee,
waiter, vendor and beggar was a potential or actual police
informer who would report on anyone he came into contact
with. To refuse to do so would have resulted in the can-
cellation of one's working or business permit or worse. In
this way the GIA and Secret Police found it easy to keep

track of almost everyone's activities at almost all times. Naturally the information obtained in this way was not always reliable. In many cases informers who had nothing of importance to report simply fabricated items of information to gain favour with the police. In other instances, people were denounced for reasons of personal revenge. In cases of denunciation the procedure was to arrest and torture first and to check facts afterwards, if at all.

Hidden microphones and phone tapping devices were a matter of routine installation in most of the Europeans' houses and apartments. I vividly recall how, when I rented my first flat in Rue Ismail Mohammad, in the Zamalek quarter, an American who turned out to be the vice-consul of the US Consulate in Cairo called on me. He explained that he had been the previous tenant, and then proceeded to show me a microphone concealed in the mouthpiece of my telephone. I disconnected it and the following day a telephone engineer appeared to check on the connection and put things right again.

On another occasion my wife and I were invited to the home of a close friend, a Dutchman named Hank Wenckebach, who was Director General of the Shell Company in Cairo. As we entered the lounge of his luxurious villa he took us over to the bar for a drink remarking, 'Now don't say anything for a minute.' Then with a grin he pushed aside a large mirror on the wall behind the bar and revealed a hidden microphone. He cursed colourfully in Arabic and tore it off. 'Now we can talk freely,' he said, 'somebody will probably be along tomorrow to repair it.'

During our stay in Egypt, my wife and I had always to keep in mind the possibility of hidden microphones, and to check our home for them. We worked out a private code which we hoped would confuse unwanted listeners. Thus we always referred to Israel as Switzerland, to Israeli Intelligence as Uncle Otto, to transmitting as 'having a go at it', and so on. Open and frank conversations on delicate

subjects were generally held in the open air where there
was no chance of being overheard.

Egyptian internal security was, and still is, among the most
active and ruthless in the world. External espionage was
another matter: it was both inefficient and badly co-
ordinated. There was an intelligence unit concentrated on
Israel, a unit concerned with the training of guerrillas for
Aden, a unit concerned with kidnapping enemy agents, and
so on. Both personnel and vast sums of money were de-
ployed in such far-ranging projects as the proposed assassina-
tions or depositions of various celebrities, including King
Saud of Saudi Arabia, his brother King Feisal, King Hassan
of Morocco, King Hussein of Jordan, President Habib Bour-
guiba of Tunis and King Idris of Libya. More money and
time were spent on financing Arab revolutions in both Arab
countries and Africa. But despite all this the GIA was
nowhere near as active abroad as it was at home. Without
the 'public eye' system it was lost. GIA agents abroad were
not always effective.

Internal counter-espionage was something that would later
consistently amuse me. For Egypt was not only flooded with
its own domestic agents carefully scrutinizing the activities
of their own countrymen, but also with literally hordes
of foreign agents carefully scrutinizing both Egyptian
domestic agents and Egyptian citizens, civil servants, government officials and ministers. Cairo and even Alexandria were,
and still are, like a giant intelligence bazaar. Everybody is
watching everybody else – and either getting paid for it or
doing it under duress. Ex-nationals, such as the German
aircraft technologists and rocket builders, must at some stage
have been wined and dined by the Egyptian Secret Police,
by Military Intelligence, by the GIA, the CIA, by the
Israeli Secret Service, the British Secret Service and by
many other intelligence organizations. But these were not
the only ones to be courted: half the Egyptian civil service
and government were infiltrated by these bodies at one time

or another. Sometimes the intelligence organizations courted each other and it would not have been uncommon to see the CIA entertaining the GIA to lunch – and certainly not uncommon to see, at any high level Egyptian social gathering, a representative from the GIA, a representative from the Israeli Secret Service and maybe a representative from the CIA. This was the kind of world I was going into – a network of plot and counterplot, a world surrounded by eyes and ears that were impossible to hide from. As I made preparations to leave for Germany and for the start of my mission to Cairo, I realized only vaguely just what kind of many-headed creature I was up against.

2

Indiscretion

I spent a year in Germany establishing my cover. I acted the part of a former German Wehrmacht officer, a nationalistic German who was readily critical of the new Germany. I stayed first in Berlin, where I joined a Riding Club, and then in Munich, changing addresses frequently. In late December 1960 it seemed safe to move ahead with the second stage of the plan. I drove overland to Genoa and there loaded the car on to an Italian liner and, on a first-class ticket, arrived in Egypt six days later. I was to pose as a tourist – a wealthy German horsebreeder.

It was good to be in Egypt at last – and at work. Yet there was one factor, one problem, that remained: loneliness. Staying in the Zahra Hotel I felt completely alone – out of my depth – and miserable. Yet I was determined to shrug it off and began at once to look around for contacts.

They weren't difficult to find. The whole aura of Egypt was a living illustration of the intensive briefing I had undergone in Israel – as if a picture had suddenly sprung to life. As I walked the streets I could immediately detect the 'public eye', the corner stone of the GIA: the Egyptian people. They sat on every corner, outside every door, outside every shop – idly watching. Their communal retina was something that was intrinsically part of the Cairo streets, the hubbub of the coffee houses, the chatter of the stories, the hustling on the pavements. It was as if the whole city was a slumberous, watchful animal.

The obvious thing for me, as a horseman, was to get an introduction to one of the local riding clubs – something the manager at the Zahra was only too delighted to arrange. The nearest, and incidentally the best, was the Cavalry Club in Gezirah which was run and maintained by Egyptian cavalry officers – though foreign visitors were welcome too. The manager of the Zahra insisted on driving me there personally, swinging into the club as noisily and as ostentatiously as he could. I got out of his car and began to stroll around, looking over the horses in their boxes and watching some riders in the paddock.

Almost immediately I was approached by a dark-skinned, clean-shaven Egyptian in riding habit who introduced himself effusively as Youssef Ali Ghorab – General of Police and Honorary President of the club. I explained to General Ghorab that I was a German tourist who had just arrived in Cairo and that since I was an enthusiastic horseman with a great love for Arabian thoroughbreds I hoped he wouldn't mind my looking round his beautiful club. I mentioned that in Germany I bred horses in a small way.

The General seemed delighted to make my acquaintance, and after an elaborate tour of inspection he invited me to have coffee with him. Soon other Egyptian riders, including some officers in uniform, joined us in the club house and were introduced to me by the General. I could hardly suppress a smile when he extravagantly explained to the others in Arabic (which I was not supposed to understand) that his good friend here was the greatest breeder and trainer of horses in the whole of Germany!

One of the ladies present, Madame Wigdane El-Barbary, whom they all called Danny, mentioned that she was giving a small cocktail party at her house that evening and would

be honoured if I came. I accepted readily and during the
next few days invitations began to flow in – the more so
when I hinted that I might eventually settle down in Egypt.

General Ghorab and I rode together daily and soon became good friends. Without much difficulty he persuaded
me to buy some horses and stable them at the club. Gradually
I became known as his protégé and acquired a large circle
of influential acquaintances.

Before long I was a regular guest at the General's home
and proceeded to cement our friendship by discreetly pre-
senting him and his family with various expensive and expected gifts. There was no doubt about it. The Egyptians
were like greedy, avaricious children. But I knew that if I
failed to keep them sweet they could easily cut up rough.
In return for my gifts Youssef Ghorab used his influence
and authority on my behalf. An introduction here, a telephone call there, licenses, permits, recommendations – they
all served the real purpose of my stay in Egypt very well
indeed. He had his own code of honour and pointed out to
me at every opportunity just how straight and honest he
was. Accepting a gift now and then, or doing a friend a
favour, were acts of friendship and had nothing to do –
heaven forbid – with bribery and corruption. Whenever
Youssef borrowed money from me, as he did occasionally,
he always insisted on returning it.

As I got to know more Egyptians I began to realize how
much I liked Youssef – he had more integrity than most and
over the next few months I started to regret not just the
way I used him but what his ultimate fate might be as a
result of our friendship.

*   *   *

Six months later, with identity and contacts firmly established, I returned to Europe – where at a sheltered rendezvous in Paris I met up again with my Israeli boss who was
well pleased with both my cover and progress.

I handed over a detailed report, together with some interesting documents and photos, and in turn received further operational instructions, a large sum of money and a tiny new transmitter that was cleverly concealed in the hollow heel of a riding boot. I was also given a code book whose key was on a page of a book about horse breeding. I was now ready to begin work in earnest – my immediate objectives being to locate Egyptian fortifications, to assess the military build-up, and to fully investigate the impending arrival of the German and Austrian aircraft and rocket constructors.

On the morning of June 3, 1961, a few minutes before eight, I boarded the Orient Express, choosing a compartment occupied by a tall, extremely pretty blue-eyed blonde with the kind of curvacious figure I always had a weakness for. There is nothing like a long boring train journey to bring people together and although she returned my initial overtures reservedly we were soon engaged in animated conversation. It turned out she was from Heilbronn in Southern Germany and that after graduating from a Swiss hotel school she had taken a job in Los Angeles as assistant manager of a large hotel. Her name was Waltraud, and she was on holiday now, visiting her parents. I told her I was a horse-breeder living in Egypt, which was close enough to the truth.

The eleven-hour train journey passed in a flash and when she got off at Stuttgart I knew I had to see her again. A few days later, in response to my barrage of telephone calls, Waltraud came to Munich, where we were together for two weeks. At the end of those two weeks we were madly in love and under normal circumstances I would have asked her to marry me; but the circumstances were anything but normal. I was under orders to proceed to Egypt almost immediately to look over Nasser's armoury – and in my job it was duty before pleasure, duty before private life, duty before personal happiness. I toyed with the idea of phoning my chief. But what would I tell him – that I had fallen in

love with a girl I had known for two weeks and would he
mind if I took her to Cairo with me? I knew what he would
say to that – and rightly so. It was preposterous.

*   *   *

Three weeks later I was driving along the autobahn
through upper Bavaria and into Austria, my foot pressed
hard on the accelerator. But 110 kilometres per hour was my
Volkswagen's limit. I had often considered buying a larger
and more expensive car, but I had seen what happened to
them in Egypt. Few cars would run on the 60-octane petrol
sold there as Super Special. So my sturdy little Volkswagen
suited me fine.

How I enjoyed that drive through the mountains and
sloping fields of upper Bavaria – the more so since on the
seat beside me, softly humming to herself and resting her
head on my shoulder from time to time, was Waltraud, my
brand new wife. I tried to look objectively at what had
happened but had to admit that of all my indiscretions this
was the one least likely to amuse my boss. Of all the deadly
sins that tempted secret agents, I had no doubt fallen victim
to the deadliest. It was a cliché-ridden, fictional situation.
Not only had I taken a wife without the knowledge, let
alone consent, of my superiors, I had also disclosed to her
my identity and my line of business – in general terms, of
course, and with no details, but she nevertheless knew now
who I was and had readily agreed to share my life – indeed
she was thrilled at the prospect of a little espionage. As a
trainee I had been warned and lectured time and again
about the perils of women for the agent. Examples of in-
discreet agents who had been caught through their women
had been given. It did not even have to be intentional.
Sometimes a woman's careless word or remark, made in all
innocence, might be sufficient to lead an agent to the firing
squad or the gallows. The courts of the Arab countries were

especially keen on death sentences. Some fun and relaxation with the opposite sex was one thing, but an involvement of this kind was taboo. I knew I had acted against the rules of logic and conscience.

I looked at Waltraud, who had cuddled up in her seat and fallen deeply asleep. I had no doubts in my mind about her, and subsequent events proved me right. Yet there was no denying that I had picked just about the worst possible moment to marry – the eve of a major mission. Sooner or later my chief was bound to find out, and I would be in the hot seat. I had to play for time in order to convince him that it was actually to my advantage to be married, that it would aid my work, that a married couple would arouse far less suspicion than a forty-year-old bachelor living alone in Cairo – and that it would also be far easier for a married couple to maintain the respectable and sound life on which my mission depended. Once the chief saw that all was going well and that my wife was actually a great asset, he would accept the 'fait accompli' – or so I hoped.

Our honeymoon was spent partly in Vienna, where Waltraud, who had never been near a horse before, fell in love with the wonderful stallions of the Spanish Riding School. From Vienna we travelled on through the Austrian lakes, finally reaching Venice where I was to embark. Waltraud was to go back to Germany to settle her affairs and join me in Egypt in about three weeks' time.

On our last night in Venice we sat on the terrace of the Hotel Danieli, looking out over the Grand Canal and drinking champagne. All that evening I had the impression that something was weighing heavily on Waltraud's mind, something more than our imminent parting. Finally, she could contain herself no longer. 'Wolfgang,' she burst out suddenly, 'I have to ask you something important. I know I promised not to ask unnecessary questions about your work and, as you said, it's better and safer for me not to know everything. But there's one thing I have to know – the country you're working for. Just tell me – is it for any of the Eastern Block countries? Russia, Eastern Germany, any of those?'

'No, certainly not. I'd never work for any of those, not for anything in the world.'

'I believe you, darling, and that's all I wanted to know.'

'And if I had been working for, say Russia, what would you have said?'

'I wouldn't have said anything, I'd simply have left you. You mustn't forget, Wolfgang, that I come from Eastern Germany, the part that is now called the German Democratic Republic. I know what Communism is like and had you been working for a Communist country – well, that would have been the end Wolfgang, much as I love you.'

'Anyway, you can put your mind at rest now. As a matter of fact, I'm working for Israel.'

'Israel!' She reflected for a while and then said, 'You know, I think that's rather nice. I'm glad. In Los Angeles I knew a girl from Israel. She never stopped talking about her country. She was so terribly proud of it. It sounds like quite a place. Don't you think the occasion warrants another bottle of champagne? Let's drink to Israel and to the success of your mission – our mission – whatever it might turn out to be.'

*   *   *

As the ship entered Alexandria harbour its loudspeakers declaimed: 'Ladies and Gentlemen, your attention please. It is strictly prohibited to take photographs of Alexandria harbour. I repeat, it is strictly prohibited to take photographs of Alexandria harbour. Anyone doing so may be arrested by the Egyptian police and have his camera confiscated. Thank you very much, Ladies and Gentlemen.'

'Good old Egypt,' I thought. 'I'm home again.' I looked at my watch. Seven fourteen. There were at least another two hours of formalities to be gone through before we docked. The pilot had to come aboard together with the health authorities. There was also passport control in the dining-room. All these activities were slow and showed a great thoroughness and devotion to duty. Only after the last passenger had been cleared would we be allowed off the ship and into the customs! I hoped to God that Youssef had received my cable and was waiting for me at the port. It would prove extremely useful to have him on hand when going through the customs. Not that I had much to worry about. Those few articles – like the transmitter in my riding boot – which really wouldn't bear close scrutiny were so well concealed that the chances of discovery were one in a thousand. What did bother me a little were all those presents I had in my luggage. No less than eight out of my seventeen suitcases and crates contained gifts for my Egyptian friends. It would have been rather difficult to explain to a customs inspector in Alexandria the reason for having five electric mixers, nine electric razors, twelve automatic Swiss watches, three tape-recorders, and so on.

Now the public system was blaring again: 'Will all passengers disembarking at Alexandria kindly proceed to the third-class dining-room for passport inspection.'

I looked over the side. A police motor launch containing six police officers and several aides was making fast. A rope ladder was lowered and, assisted by a couple of sailors, they all climbed aboard. Here they were received by the purser, whose professionally cordial greeting they returned with dignity. They proceeded to the third-class dining-room. I strolled along behind them. One was a lieutenant-colonel, one a major, the rest captains. All were dressed in the smart white and gold of the port police, were swarthy of face and uniformly moustached. The aides wore ill-fitting, none-too-clean khaki drill and black down-at-heel army boots. Their job was to carry the ledgers which contained the so-called black lists. Recorded there in alphabetical order were the names of persons who were to be denied entry into the United Arab Republic, or to be arrested on arrival. People who had criminal or political records, or were simply under suspicion. I hoped my name had not suddenly been included.

I entered the third-class dining-room in the wake of the police. The room was crowded with passengers waiting to get their examination over. The ship's air-conditioning system could not cope with so much perspiring humanity: you could cut the air with a knife. More passengers from outside were trying to push into the already over-crowded room. The procedure is long and complicated. A soldier hands you a printed form to be filled in in duplicate. The demands include – name, nationality, passport number, home address, profession, religion, purpose of your visit to Egypt, details of previous visits, persons you knew in Egypt, and so on. Having completed this literary exercise you give the form, together with your passport, to the captain at the first table. He scrutinizes the whole affair slowly and carefully, perhaps asks a few clarifying questions, stamps your paper and passes it on to captain number two. Captain number two reads it all once more, compares the details with those in your passport, initials your form and hands it across to the third captain. He is the one with the ledgers. He looks you deep in the eye, then reads your passport from beginning to end, looks up again and asks your name. He checks your passport to see if you have told the truth and now asks captain number four to hand him a specific ledger. By joint effort this is opened at the appropriate page and together they read all the names on that page. Two forefingers run down it all the way. Up again. Once more, down again. Nothing. Your form is initialled and retained. Your passport is sent across the room by special constable to the major who stamps it twice without looking at it and returns it to you. The lieutenant-colonel presides and supervises. Inspection over. Thank you very much. You may go. The whole procedure takes about fifteen minutes.

I decided to stroll around the deck while the crowd in the dining-room thinned out. In any case we wouldn't dock before all the passengers had been examined. Time enough for a short walk in the fresh air and a cigarette. Pulled by a tug we were just moving very slowly into the harbour area, making for the main quay in front of the customs. Already I could make out the well-remembered bustle of activity at the quayside. Hundreds of people preparing to receive the incoming ship. Gangs of porters clad in rags, getting ready to rush aboard the minute the first plank was thrown across. Clearing agents who made their living by having connections in the lower echelons of customs officials and who could usually manage, for a small consideration, to get you off the ship and through the customs formalities a little faster than it took normally. There were husky stevedores to unload cars, heavy luggage and freight. Taxi drivers, hotel porters, travel agents, photographers, carters, hawkers, musicians, acrobats. The Public Eye – all earning a living of sorts from selling wares, themselves, or information on other people.

Suddenly the public address system blared again: 'Will Signor Lotz please come to the first-class salon. I repeat, Signor Lotz...' Someone knew. Then I dismissed the thought as quickly as it had come. Most likely they wanted to return to me something I had mislaid or forgotten. But why do that in the first-class salon and not in the purser's office?

Puzzled, and a little wary, I took a short cut across B deck, up the ladder and through the bar into the first-class salon. It was empty except for the purser who was having a whisky with two Egyptian police officers – the lieutenant-colonel and one of the captains from passport control. They rose as I entered and the lieutenant-colonel addressed me in fairly good English:

'Do I have the pleasure of speaking to Mr Lotz?'

'That's my name,' I replied. 'What can I do for you?'

C

He came to attention, threw me a salute and then shook my hand warmly.

'I am Colonel Abdel Aziz Metwally. I have just received a message from General Youssef Ghorab asking me to welcome you and to put my services at your disposal. The General will be on the dock. He came specially from Cairo.' He gave me a searching look. 'You must be very good friends.'

'Oh yes,' I replied, 'we've known each other for quite a while. It's a great honour to be numbered among the General's close friends.' He got the message. Springing to attention once more, he said:

'The General has asked me to look after you, Sir. May I have your passport?'

I handed it over. He turned to the captain and barked in Arabic:

'Stamp this right away.'

My passport was stamped with great care and returned to me with a flourish and a polite 'etfaddal effendim'.

'Alf Shoukr ya bey,' I thanked him. The colonel intervened:

'Ah you speak Arabic? How clever of you.'

'Not really,' I replied, 'just a few words I picked up.'

'What about your luggage?' he asked. 'Is it all in your cabin?'

'Only the small bags. The heavier pieces are in the hold. Also my car. Perhaps it would be best to have an agent handle it.'

He reacted as I knew he would: 'That is out of the question. We shall handle everything for you. Why spend good money on one of those useless agents? It would be an insult to the General. Just leave it all to me.'

He saluted and left. Ten minutes later he was replaced by my friend – the General himself. Musingly I watched him come up the gangway. He was surrounded by officers and he marched at their front in all his splendour, complete with four rows of medals and shining brass all over him. He was clean-shaven, with a sallow skin and was about forty-five years old. He was followed by three full colonels in similar, if somewhat less impressive, attire.

Youssef enjoyed being a general and he acted the part to perfection. Yet he was known as a hard worker and efficient administrator and greatly feared by his subordinates for his severity. Almost twenty-five years of service in the police – many of them in senior posts – had left their mark on him. Where others walked, he strutted. Where others relaxed, he maintained inflexible dignity, and anything he had to say was delivered with an air of handing down a royal decree. Moreover, he had a reputation for being honest – that's why I liked him. While others in similar positions had amassed fortunes through bribery and favouritism, he had no personal means and was often in financial difficulties. On the other hand – being an Egyptian – there was nothing he loved more than pomp, ceremony and gifts. He made a great show of being a fervent nationalist and Gamal Abdul Nasser was his idol – just as King Farouk had been before him.

'Rusty, my friend, my dear friend, welcome home to Egypt.'

Now the inevitable happened, as I knew it would: he embraced me, then kissed me on both cheeks and on the lips.

'Wahashteni,' he said in Arabic, 'I have missed you! We have all missed you,' he added with a sweeping movement of his arm, presumably referring to the populace as a whole. 'But you have returned.'

Not to be outdone I replied with an old Egyptian proverb: 'He who has once drunk from the water of the Nile shall always return.' I almost smiled as I said it but managed by great self-discipline to refrain.

Youssef beamed. 'You learned that from me and you have not forgotten it. Now let me introduce these officers. Colonel Mistikawy, the port commander (salute, handshake)

– Colonel Rashidi (salute, handshake) – Colonel Said (salute, handshake). I suggest we get off this crowded deck and have a coffee in the commandant's office while we wait for your things. Unloading the car may take a little time.'

We went across the decks, down the gangway and into the main building with two police constables running ahead, clearing the way. As soon as we were seated the port commandant clapped his hands and ordered coffee. I turned to Youssef: 'Your Colonel Metwally has been extremely helpful with my luggage.' Then, with a meaningful look I added, 'I've brought a great many things.'

'Good, good,' he replied, 'I'm glad he was of help. Will all the luggage fit in your car?

'I'm afraid not. There is rather a lot of it.'

'Maalesh – it doesn't matter. I shall send it to Cairo in a police truck.'

'That's good of you. I'm anxious to get back to Cairo today.'

'Then you'd better come in my car and I'll let my driver take yours. But first we must lunch together at the Alexandria officers' club. By the way, Abdo phoned me this morning. They are throwing a welcoming party for you tonight at his place in Heliopolis!'

'So it will be a wild night. You know Abdo and his crowd.'

'Why worry? You can sleep it off tomorrow.'

That's what he thought. I had to transmit at six. Just a short message this time: ARRIVED SAFELY, ALL IS WELL.

The General extended his monogrammed silver cigarette case (a present from me with compliments of the Israeli Intelligence) and we both lit up.

'Well, Rusty, it's certainly good to have you back. Tell me about your trip. What's new?'

'Not much. Among other things I got married. My wife will be here in a couple of weeks. Will you send her flowers?'

'Why that's quite fantastic – but here comes the Captain

with your car keys and the documents. Let's go. I must
hear all about this marriage of yours over lunch.'

*   *   *

Three weeks later I drove Waltraud from Alexandria to
Cairo. I had missed her bitterly; the weeks away from her
had been considerably worse than the long lonely months
before I met her.

Coming from Alexandria in the afternoon with the sun
behind you, and after driving through 240 kilometres of
barren desert, the picture that presents itself to the traveller
is incredible. I had come this way before but now I stopped
the car and we both got out to have a better look. Below
us the yellow desert gave way dramatically to an area of
voluptuous green vegetation. There was no gradual transi-
tion. The borderline between sterile desert and rich, cultivated land seemed as if carved out with a knife. The pyramids
were on our right. To our left, framed by palms trees, groves
and plantations, lay Cairo, its ancient domes, towers and
minarets blending strangely with modern skyscrapers. Waltraud was bewildered.

'That's what you get in exchange for Los Angeles,' I said
to her.

'The mysterious East,' she smiled. 'It looks beautiful and
dangerous.'

Entering the outskirts of the city, passing Mena House
– once considered among the best and most elegant hotels
in Cairo, but now beginning to look shabby with disrepair
– I turned left into Pyramid Road, a major traffic artery
running from the foot of the pyramids to the suburb of
Giza, a distance of some fifteen kilometres. Now Waltraud
could see the true squalor and poverty of the city. She was
also amazed at the traffic on the roads. Vehicles of all kinds
– most of them old beaten-up affairs of ancient vintage –
were moving at surprising speed through a mass of pedes-

trians, donkey carts, camels and water buffaloes. None of them, apparently was observing traffic rules of any description.

She looked up at me horrified. 'It *is* dangerous,' she said.

'Dangerous in lots of ways,' I grinned.

We went through Giza, past the zoo, across one of the wide bridges spanning the Nile, and entered Zamalek. Here the buildings were newer, the streets cleaner, and the traffic less dense. There were modern shops and a considerable number of Europeans could be seen driving new cars with foreign number plates. I drew up at the entrance of number sixteen Sharia Ismail Mohammad. The two Sudanese boabs rushed down the steps of the marble doorway to take our luggage. These boabs, or doorkeepers, were a time-honoured institution, probably as old as Egypt itself. Every respectable household had at least one. Their job was mainly to stand at the entrance, prevent thieves and beggars from entering, act as porters and messengers and carry out minor repairs around the house. They were also part of the public eye – and like most servants acted as police spies. Once a week or so they reported to the secret police on everything that went on in the house: how the tenants lived, how they spent their money, what they spoke about among themselves, who came to visit them, what mail they received, and so on. Every little detail had to be reported. Many of them, especially the Sudanese, who had a reputation for loyalty, did their informing most unwillingly and only under threat.

Going up in the lift I said to Waltraud: 'We shall probably have a full house tonight. Most of my friends have heard of your arrival and they will all be coming to say hello. They are dying to meet you.'

She was taken aback. 'My God, look at the state of my hair ... How am I expected to prepare food for so many people at a moment's notice.'

Reassuringly I told her the servants would cope with the refreshments and that she could show off her superior cooking another night – I also told her we could speak freely since I had checked everywhere for microphones.

My living-room looked like a flower shop. Baskets of different shapes and sizes containing elaborate flower arrangements stood on every available piece of furniture. There was no doubt as to the success of my contacts system.

'Let's see who sent all these,' I said to Waltraud, and together we examined the cards pinned to the baskets. We began with the biggest: "We are honoured to greet the bride of our esteemed friend Lotz" – signed: "Youssef Ali Ghorab, General of Police, and family." Of course, dear old Youssef. I told you about him, darling. Let's see the next one. "A thousand welcomes to the fair lady of Rusty Bey. You may come to like our Nile water when slightly diluted with whisky – Abdel Salaam Suleiman, General!" He's a joker. We are good friends and I rather like him.'

'Another General?' Waltraud asked.

'Oh, there are millions of them in Egypt. This one has quite a head on his shoulders. Lived in England for years and something rubbed off on him. He does not even think like an Egyptian any more. He is a logistics expert. Very important to me.'

'You mean he gives you military information?'

'Frequently. But he doesn't know it. Let's see the other cards. This one is in German. Ah yes – "Looking forward to meeting you – Nadia and Franz Kiesow." That's a couple you'll like. He's a German, local representative of Mannesmann. Prepares reports for them on the market and economy here. Been in the country for years and is married to an Eygptian. They love to live it up. – Who's this? Another one in German: "Respects – Gerhard Bauch." Just like him! Always the German ex-officer. He's supposed to be the local manager of a big German concern. Owns a lovely villa at the Pyramid Gardens. Keeps a horse in the club – terrible rider. But there's something else about him too. He's not true to type for a salesman, even a big salesman. He's just

a little too free with his money, lives just a little too elegantly, and has just a little too much time on his hands
which he spends sightseeing and going to parties. What's
more, he doesn't seem to be doing any business. There's
something fishy about him.'

Waltraud said that he sounded like a spy and I laughed
confidently saying: 'I've thought of that. Better be careful
of him. We can't afford to get mixed up with spies of all
people.'

'I should hope not. But you live in style too, and you are
certainly not stingy with money. Doesn't that arouse anybody's suspicion?'

'No, I am pretty sure it doesn't. On the contrary, it
achieves its purpose. The difference between me and all
these foreign commercial representatives is this: They are
supposed to make a living here. They receive a fixed salary
plus a certain percentage on the deals they make. It's easy
for the Egyptian authorities to check on their earnings. If
they spend more money than they earn, it stands to reason
that they have an additional income of some kind. Either
they smuggle currency, as some of them do (especially the
Embassy people), or else they make money in some other
way. And that – as you say – provokes suspicion. With me
it's quite different. I'm supposed to be a rich man back
home. If the Egyptians ask any of my acquaintances in
Germany – they all know I'm wealthy. Nobody can check
my German bank accounts. I might have millions for all
they know. I live here to breed Arab horses, which is considered an elegant hobby for a gentleman of means. Not only
can I spend as much money as I want with impunity – but
they expect me to do it. There is nothing Egyptians love
more than ostentation.'

I looked at Waltraud to see how she was taking all this.
I was making it sound so easy. But talking to her
and surrounded by the flowers – that was the way it
seemed.

I glanced at the next batch. 'Brigadier-General Fouad Osman and Colonel Mohsen Said. Ah yes, they'll probably be coming to look you over tonight. Army Intelligence, both of them. I see them often.'

My confidence was increasing – she was wonderful therapy for me. A much-needed sounding board. And she was asking all the right questions – even down to how I squeezed my influential friends for information. I replied easily: 'Well, I certainly don't walk up to them and ask them for it. That would be a little too crude. And trying to buy the information from them outright would be far too risky. But all Egyptians are talkative by nature. Any person who likes to talk a lot will sooner or later say something which would best remain unsaid. My system is to get several of them together at a party, give them a damn good meal and plenty of whisky – which most of them love but can't afford to buy – and then they soon start talking among themselves about matters concerning their military duties. You'd be surprised what one can get out of such casual conversations.'

I knew that, as far as Waltraud was concerned, I was dealing with a beginner – and that I would have to teach her the ABC of living in the Orient, as well as the subtleties of my work.

'The drink makes them careless. It's all so damned simple. Another thing is that they don't realize that I speak Arabic. They think I know only a few simple phrases and they feel quite free to talk in front of me on subjects they would not mention before others. But sometimes when I get one of them alone, he will also speak to me about secret or confidential matters. That's because they like to show off. Most of them have a terrible inferiority complex, and all the time they have to prove to themselves and to others how big and important they are and how much they know. They all think I was an officer in Rommel's Afrika Korps and so love to discuss military subjects with me. The fact that I am on intimate terms with a few big shots around here places me automatically above suspicion in security matters. Some of them even seek my professional advice.

'Naturally I don't accept everything they say at face value. But it shows me where to look. Let's say I get a certain piece of information that interests me. In that case I have to create an opportunity to speak to at least one or two other people who are likely to have this information too. At a suitable moment I introduce the subject into the conversation as discreetly as possible and wait and see what happens. If they confirm the information, or the main points of it, I can safely regard it as accurate and report to headquarters accordingly. Also, if, for instance, somebody tells me the location of an important military installation, I may have to go there and see for myself.'

Suddenly Waltraud exclaimed: 'You really do enjoy this, don't you?'

'Well, doesn't everybody enjoy doing things he believes are worthwhile? If I worried all the time about being unmasked I'd be a nervous wreck by now. It's just like a soldier at the front-line who thinks of nothing but being hit by a bullet or a shell. He's no good for anything and is usually among the first to be killed.'

I went on to explain how in this kind of work there was no doing things by half measures, how you couldn't be squeamish, how you had to do things which, by accepted moral standards, were questionable, how you had to pretend friendship for people you hated and despised, how – even worse – you sometimes had to make use of people you had befriended and really liked. After all, it was war, and war was not a game.

Shortly after ten o'clock our guests began to arrive. It was a common custom in Egypt for social functions to take place fairly late and to last until the small hours of the morning. The first to come was Danny. She rushed in, in her usual whirlwind manner, embracing both of us and wishing us luck. So far so good. I had been a little uncertain about her reaction to my sudden marriage – for she had had her eyes on me as a prospective husband from the moment I first met her at the Cavalry Club. Luckily discretion had kept me out of her clutches.

Danny – Madame Wigdane El-Barbary – was actually the wife of a prominent and very wealthy physician. A typical, somewhat exaggerated, example of the modern emancipated Egyptian woman, she had of course been one of my earliest acquaintances in Cairo. Horses, of which she owned several, were her main hobby, and she was a keen rider and active member of the Cavalry Club. Most of her friends were Europeans of both sexes.

The Egyptians had little understanding or sympathy for an independent woman who rode horses, who went to parties unescorted by her husband and generally conducted herself like a foreigner. The story of her life was no secret to anyone who knew her even slightly. She was now in her mid-thirties and had been married in name only to an Egyptian for over fifteen years. There was nothing that she and her husband had in common. They had even given up all pretence of having a normal marriage. Moving in different social sets they both went their own way and, while still living under the same roof, would sometimes evade each other for weeks.

Now I had returned from a short trip abroad, happily married to a brand-new wife, and Danny had come to greet her. Under ordinary circumstances I wouldn't have cared a damn about her reactions, but in this job I had to avoid alienating people as far as possible. I was here to make friends, not enemies. But she showed no sign of jealousy. In fact she was overdoing it a bit, kissing Waltraud again and again and showering her with compliments.

The others were coming in now in groups of twos and threes. Most of them were men. Egyptians were not, as a rule, in the habit of taking their wives to social functions. Besides, many of those present were unmarried. The living-room was soon filled with guests, all talking at once in Arabic or English, greeting one another with a great deal of back-slapping and noisy laughter. My servant, Zaki, assisted by two hired waiters, kept everybody supplied with drinks. Waltraud stood surrounded by a group of my closer friends who had just arrived, among them Abdel Salaam, called Abdo for short, with his bosom pal, General Fouad Osman, Chief of Security for rocket bases and military factories. Also there were Franz Kiesow and his wife Nadia. I jostled through the crowd to greet them.

'Never mind introducing us to your wife,' Nadia called out to me, 'we've already introduced ourselves.' She kissed me. 'Rusty, you old pirate, where did your get yourself such a lovely wife? You don't deserve anything like this!'

'I quite agree, Nadia my love. How are you, Franz?'

'Oooh – business as usual, which means lousy – whisky prices going up all the time – Nadia spending money left and right – in other words, situation normal. Nothing to com-plain about.'

On it went. Compliments, banter, drinking – more com-pliments, more banter, more drinking. And all the time I was waiting for snippits of information to emerge with the drink and the chat.

Youssef Ghorab entered the room, smiling and waving in a restrained, dignified way. Noticing our group he changed direction and strutted up to us. I braced myself for the obligatory brotherly kiss. That over, I introduced him to Waltraud. He kissed her hand elegantly and recited in broken German some of the words of a bawdy drinking song I had once written down for him at his request when we had both attended a German Fasching party. He had learned them by heart and, probably thinking they were the last word in classical German poetry, he recited them at every opportunity. His actual knowledge of the German language was limited to this particular rhyme and a couple of others which were even worse. Franz Kiesow had heard it from him before, but Waltraud, I noticed, found it extremely difficult to keep a straight face.

I turned to my other guests. The folding doors to the dining-room, where a cold buffet was laid out, were thrown open and they all helped themselves to the roast beef, turkey, stuffed pigeons and many other delicacies which had been prepared and sent over by Groppi's catering department.

The evening wore on as most evenings of this kind do. Waltraud and Youssef Ghorab came over to me arm-in-arm, already the best of friends.

'What are your plans for tomorrow?' Youssef asked. 'Will I see you at the club in the morning?'

'By all means,' I replied. 'My wife is having her first riding lesson.'

'I shall be there all morning,' Youssef said. 'I will also ride and introduce the members to Mrs Lotz.'

He went on to ask us to join him and his wife for drinks the next evening. 'We'd love to,' I replied quickly, 'but could we postpone it till the day after? I have already accepted an invitation for tomorrow night. Von Leers is giving a party.' And I certainly wasn't going to miss that. Von Leers, who was an ex-deputy of Goebbels, had been included in my briefing. I was sure to meet some valuable ex-Nazi contacts at his house.

'I met the Professor once.' Youssef was saying. 'A most cultured old gentleman. All right, Rusty, so my family and I will expect you the day after tomorrow.'

'And tomorrow night you come to us,' intervened Franz Kiesow, who in passing had overheard the last part.

'I am sorry, Franz, I was just telling Youssef Bey that we are engaged tomorrow. The Von Leers party. Won't you be there?'

'Me? Not likely! I don't mix with that crowd, too many Nazis.'

I did not reply. Youssef looked a little pained. Gerhard Bauch, who had been standing nearby, joined us. He smiled his little-boy smile, clicked his heels and bowed to Waltraud. 'Compliments, gnä' Frau. Lovely party.' Then to me: 'I hear you are on visiting terms with Von Leers. Always wanted to meet that man. Do you think you can get me an introduction? I'd be very much obliged.' That Bauch – he didn't miss much!

'Yes, I suppose I could manage an introduction.'

I couldn't very well refuse him. But what did he want with Von Leers? All the other representatives of German firms in Cairo avoided the prominent old ex-Nazi like the plague.

Youssef seemed anxious to avoid any involvement in a controversy between Germans regarding Nazism. I knew how much he sympathized with the Nazis, but he owed it to his position not to say so in public. He now asked about my plans to take Waltraud sightseeing. I replied that first I wanted her to settle down in her new home and meet my friends, and that then, gradually, I would start taking her on trips and showing her the sights and places of historical interest.

'You do that,' Youssef agreed. 'No need to go rushing around like tourists, tiring her out. You have all the time in the world. I'd love to come with you on some of those trips and show you things and places tourists never get to see. The antiquities may be very interesting, but I want to show you modern Egypt. I want to show you what has been achieved by Arab socialism, by our technical progress and by our military might.' He raved on for some time until Danny interrupted us. Disentangling myself from her I walked in Fouad's direction and heard the word 'sabotage'. Immediately I joined the group.

'Stop being so serious,' I said smoothly, 'you *are* anti-social types. I am not interrupting anything official, am I?'

'Not at all. I was just telling Abdo . . . well, I can tell you too, Rusty, but keep it to yourself. There has been an explosion in one of the military factories. Five killed.'

'Was it an accident?'

'We don't think so. It looks more like the Israelis. The stuff came from abroad in a crate of spare parts. Don't mention this to anyone. We are trying to keep it a secret.'

I nodded discreetly.

With the catalyst of alcohol, the conversation was becoming increasingly intriguing. Everyone began to split up into small groups and I found myself sitting next to my friend, General Abdel Salaam. Abdo was responsible for the movements of troops and munitions – by land, sea and air. Therefore it was important to draw him out. I turned to him:

'What have you been doing with yourself lately, Abdo? I haven't seen you for days.'

'Oh, they keep me busy. I've been running down to Suez and back all week.'

'What's so attractive about Suez?'

'Nothing. As you know it's a hell of a place. But we've been transferring an armoured brigade from here to the Canal area and, as usual, I had to play nursemaid to a bunch of incompetent staff officers.'

'Well, let me know when you're starting the war, Abdo, and I'll stock up with whisky.'

'That is *always* a good idea, though the war will have to wait a little. We have enough war materials to conquer the whole Middle East, but that isn't everything. The state of the army is scandalous.'

'It can't be as bad as all that?' I put in naïvely.

'But it is. The trouble is, Gamal and the Marshal and most of the senior Generals don't realize it. They have new Russian planes and armour but they're like a bunch of children with a new football. Even the best football is no good if the team doesn't know how to play. Sure, we have a few elite units, but one swallow doesn't make a spring. On the whole our soldiers are badly trained and their morale is low. Administration is tied up in any amount of red tape and functions far too slowly, if at all. Our field officers have no authority to make even minor decisions and our whole conception of battle tactics is antiquated.'

He beckoned to one of the waiters who was passing with a tray. 'Listen, Rusty,' he continued, 'I served in Farouk's army years ago before this glorious republic came into being. It was all spit and polish and bullshit. The Cavalry and the Royal Guard and parades with drawn swords. It was very nice and decorative, but everyone from the king down to the last stable boy knew it was not a fighting army and we were just playing at being soldiers. I know what a fighting army is and how it is run. I saw the Allied armies during the Second World War and I graduated from staff and command college in England. You are a former Nazi officer, I don't have to tell you what an efficient army is like.'

I extended my cigarette case to him and we both lit up.

'Well, Abdo,' I said, 'you are drawing a pretty black picture. You're probably over-tired. Been working too much, as usual.'

'I'm not over-tired, just disgusted with this whole bloody outfit. I have already asked three times to be pensioned. This leg of mine is excuse enough. Now they've refused for the third time. They need me in administration.'

'No wonder, the way you work. But from what I hear elsewhere, the armed forces are improving all the time. You have foreign advisers and the army had practical battle experience during the Suez war.'

'Oh yes, we have foreign advisers all right. First we had Germans, now we have Russians. We get the best foreign expert in the world to instruct us on a certain subject, and five minutes later we not only tell him what to do, but also how to do it. That's the Egyptian mentality. Look at the aircraft and rocket industries our president is so proud of. Hundreds of millions of pounds and what have we got to show for it?'

'Not much, I know.

'Everyone knows! Just as they know about our battle experience and so-called "victories" in 1956. A load of bull. I was in Sinai, I saw what happened. It was a debacle. No co-ordination of any kind, conflicting orders or no orders at all – and then we just turned and ran, officers in the lead. Now we think another two or three armoured divisions and another five hundred aircraft will do the trick next time. We look for quantity instead of military efficiency. And we will pay for it when the time comes.'

'When do you think that will be?'

'Oh, we are not going to war next week or next month. But it will come, that's certain.' He laughed and got to his feet. 'It will come as surely as I'm half drunk now and have to go home.'

I also rose, and nudging him in the ribs replied: 'Don't take it to heart, old boy. If they kick you out of the army for criticizing them all the time, I can always wangle a good job for you in Germany. That is if you can manage without your gold braid.'

'What do you mean manage without it? I'll need it if I'm to become doorman at the Berlin Hilton!'

He had regained his usual carefree and cheerful attitude. 'It's a good thing you give me an occasional shoulder to cry on,' he added with a short laugh, 'I can't talk like that at the office. They don't take kindly to criticism.'

He said goodnight to Waltraud and me, inviting us to visit him soon at his home in Heliopolis, and left, waving goodbye to the others. His limp, the result of an old injury he had received running his jeep over a landmine in Sinai, was very noticeable tonight.

*   *   *

As we got into bed I suddenly remembered my homework. I told Waltraud that I had to work. She wondered: 'Work at this hour? What's so terribly urgent?'

D

'It will only take about twenty minutes, but I have to do it now. I picked up some bits of information tonight that will interest the boys. The transfer of an armoured brigade to the Canal area might be important. I'll have to go there in a couple of days and see for myself. There were a few other things too. I'll write out a message and put it into code for transmission tomorrow morning at six. It won't take me long.'

'Can I come with you, when you go to the Canal area?'

'Why not? Might be a good idea at that. We'll take some fishing tackle and bathing suits, and for all the world we'll be nothing but a couple of tourists going for a swim in the Bitter Lakes and minding their own business. And what our real business is – nobody will suspect.'

After I had drafted out the wireless message for the next morning's transmission I gave Waltraud a few brief details about Von Leers.

'He's an old Nazi, a major war criminal. Used to be Goebbels' right-hand man. He can't go back to Germany because they would throw him into prison. Now he enjoys asylum in Egypt. The Egyptians don't consider him very important any more. They gave him a post as minor adviser in some ministry or other and pay him a meagre salary. He became a Moslem and changed his name to Omar Amin, but nobody takes it seriously and they all still call him Von Leers.'

'Why is he so important to you? Important to Bauch too, apparently.'

'He's not important to me in himself. Whatever he may have been once, he's now a senile old fool of no consequence. What interests me is not the never-ceasing recital of his reminiscences from the Third Reich, when he was a Colonel in the SS, but the people one meets at his place. Some of the top experts in the aircraft and rocket production here – Germans and Austrians. People like Brenner, Schonmann, Schwamm, Vogelsang – you'll soon meet them all. There are

others too – important men like Pilz and Stengel. Some are
not very nice, like that boor Brenner for example, who
starts belching and bawling Nazi songs after his third drink;
but being on friendly terms with them is a good way of
getting reliable information on the progress of their work.
For that I'll even belch and bawl with Brenner. It pays off.'

I explained to Waltraud how important it was to investigate the work of the German experts, to obtain accurate
and full details regarding progress on aircraft production
and rocket building – as well as general military information
relating to troop movements, armaments, state of training,
military roads, new military airfields, etc., and political information about what really went on behind the scenes.
Then I said: 'Come to think of it, Bauch may be after the
same things. I told you he was a bit of a dark horse. I often
wonder what he really does for a living.'

'Perhaps he's a colleague of yours after all, working for
a different organization. In that case, why not get together
and pool your information?'

I laughed and kissed her. 'My motto is a simple one –
never trust anybody.'

'And me – what about me?'

'You are not anybody.'

I kissed her again and turned off the light.

3

Stallions for Spying

The Nady El-Faroussia – the Cavalry Club – was situated next to the racecourse of the Gezira Sporting Club on the Nile island of Gezira, less than five minutes drive from the adjacent district of Zamalek, where we lived. It was shortly past eight when Waltraud and I arrived the next morning – a little later than was usual for me. As we passed through the ornamental iron gates on our way into the club grounds, I saw that most of the regular morning crowd were already there, riding or sipping coffee on the well-kept lawn in front of the clubhouse. To our left, in the main riding-ring, General Ghorab was exercising a lovely grey Arab mare called Boulboul, property of the club but kept for the General's personal use. Youssef cut a good figure on a horse. He was considered one of the best dressage riders in the country and was indeed an accomplished horseman, although his method of handling a horse was, as a rule, a trifle too severe for my taste. On seeing us Youssef dismounted, patted the neck of his perspiring mare, and came over.

'I was waiting for you,' he said, 'I thought we might do a few jumps together. But it seems that late nights don't agree with you,' he added with a laugh. 'Are you going to ride now?'

'I don't think so,' I replied. 'My wife is going to have her first lesson, and after that it will be too hot for anything but sitting in the shade.'

'That's true,' Youssef agreed, 'so let's arrange for the lesson now. Later she can see the club and meet the members.'

After the lesson, Ghorab and I took Waltraud to see the stables. As I showed her one of my grey stallions I remembered a story I could not possibly relate in front of Ghorab. Shortly after my arrival in Cairo I had heard at the club that a prominent racehorse owner, Ali Sharei, was selling off some of his stock. I had made it known that I was on the look-out for a good stud, and one of the club members, a Dr Mahmoud Raghab Fahmy, who was a senior official at the ministry of agriculture, had offered to take me to the farm where Sharei's horses were kept. An appointment was made and we had driven out there one afternoon. This particular stallion had taken my fancy and so I had asked about the price. Although I spoke Arabic fluently it was important to let everyone believe that I knew only a few phrases. So Dr Raghab Fahmy translated for me.

'How much do you want for this animal?' he had asked the owner in Arabic. 'A hundred and twenty pounds,' had been the prompt reply. 'All right. He is not worth more than a hundred, but since you are a friend of mine and this damn foreigner is loaded with money I'll get you the hundred and twenty pounds you ask. I'm sure you'll show your gratitude.'

Then he had turned and said to me in English: 'This man wants a lot of money, but I am here to see that you are not taken advantage of. Leave everything to me, Mr Lotz, you will not have to pay a piastre more than a hundred and seventy pounds!'

What could I do? I could have haggled over the price. I could have refused and come back another time with somebody more honest. But I needed the good offices of this official if I wanted to breed and export horses. So there was no alternative but to shut up and pay up.

Having finished our rounds of the stables, the three of us made our way to the clubhouse. It was almost ten o'clock and the heat was becoming oppressive. Nobody was riding now, and many club members were sprawling in wicker armchairs on the shady verandah, sipping coffee or iced lemonade. Waltraud already knew some of those present. Danny was giving a lecture to no one in particular on what a proper jumping seat should be like. Nadia Kiesow was there in her usual elegant riding outfit. She owned a small chestnut mare, a timid creature of which she was terrified. With Nadia sat Bauch who, as always, seemed to have all the time in the world. Youssef proceeded to introduce those whom Waltraud had not yet met: Colonel Kamal Hadidy, commandant of the police college, Colonel Mohsen Sabri, one of those who had sent Waltraud flowers but had not turned up at last night's party, and Dr Raouf Megally, an eye surgeon who was with his Australian wife, Wyn. (I had convinced Wyn that we had met in Australia – and she had been busy telling everybody else that this was so.) There were also five cavalry officers, members of the Egyptian international jumping team who, after exercising their horses for an hour or so each morning, would spend the rest of the day lolling around one or other of the sporting clubs and most of the night smoking hashish or trying to pick up girls at the Hilton or the Semiramis.

As we ordered coffee, they all drew up their chairs in a circle and the conversation became general.

'Are you planning to settle in Egypt permanently?' asked Colonel Mohsen Sabri. I was not quite sure in which branch of the intelligence service he worked, but I knew he had something to do with checking on foreign residents and that he seldom asked a question unless there was a definite purpose behind it.

' "Permanently" is a big word,' I replied, 'but if my wife likes the country as much as I do, we may well stay here for a number of years. That is, if the authorities approve.'

'Why shouldn't they,' responded Sabri quickly. 'On the contrary, we like having you with us. Vice-President Hussein El-Shafei was speaking highly of you only the other day.'

'How kind of him. Please give him my regards. I haven't had the pleasure of seeing him for some time.'

I had come into contact with El-Shafei through the Horsemen's Association of which he was Honorary President and I an active member. Politically he was zero, a Nasser yes-man of no consequence despite the fact that he was Vice-President of the Republic (an office he still holds). Behind his back he was often referred to as 'al gahash al gumhoury' – the republican donkey.

'I've just seen the racing form for this afternoon,' remarked Major Alwy Ghazy, one of the cavalry officers. 'A horse of yours is running in the fifth race, Rusty. Shall I put a fiver on him?'

'You could do worse, Alwy. Though I don't guarantee anything.'

'Who's your trainer?'

'Maurice. He's first-rate.'

'Yes, he certainly is. I've visited his stables in Heliopolis. His training track is next to the armoured corps.'

That was no coincidence either, but something I had carefully taken into account when choosing my trainer. Apart from a few armoured units in the Canal area, the Egyptian army kept practically all its armour concentrated in one huge base in the desert near Heliopolis: any major move of armoured vehicles would originate from that particular base. The track on which my trainer, Maurice, exercised the racehorses in his care each morning was right next to it. What's more, a fifteen foot high wooden observation tower had been erected in the centre of the oval track so that trainers and owners could watch their horses being exercised.

Every morning I would mount the observation tower, armed with a pair of powerful binoculars – and it was not only horses that I observed. Turning a little to the right I was able to spot almost everything that went on inside the armoured base. If tanks or armoured vehicles were moving out, I could clearly see the direction they were taking; and later I would follow in my car to check out their exact destination. Once again I realized how vital it was for Israeli Intelligence to have on the spot a trained, regular army officer like myself who had served in combat units for many years: at a glance I was able to determine the nature of a convoy, to assess whether I was watching an operational move, a unit going on manoeuvres or into training, armoured vehicles being taken to the repair shop or whatever.

'Are you going to buy some more horses soon?' Bauch was asking me.

'Certainly, though I don't know how soon. As you know, I'm planning to do some breeding on a modest scale. The other day I saw a couple of rare beauties at Hamza Pasha's farm. It seems he's willing to sell them but until I get a farm of my own I've nowhere to put them. Here at the club there isn't a single empty box.'

'Why don't you stable them with our horses at the army barracks at Abassia Rusty?' asked Major Ghazy. 'Omar, don't you think that can be arranged?'

Colonel Omar El-Hadary, commander of the cavalry unit at Abassia and chef d'équipe of the jumping team, stroked his moustache. 'I don't see why not,' he replied after a pause. 'We have plenty of room. Each of your horses would get his own soldier groom and be well taken care of. Yes, it can be arranged easily enough.'

I thanked him warmly, but pointed out that since Abassia

was an extremely large military garrison it would be impossible to visit my horses regularly, as I needed to do, and that I would always be bothering him to escort me.

He laughed. 'Rusty, how very German you are! Haven't you got passport photographs of yourself and madame? Just give them to me and I'll have passes made out for you both. Come when you like, go when you like.'

It was as simple as that. For a long time I had been eager to get inside the Abassia garrison.

Alwy Ghazy consulted his watch. 'Time to go,' he shouted, jumping to his feet. 'I have a gorgeous blonde waiting for me at the Gezira Sporting Club. An American.' The other four cavalrymen also rose and, saluting politely, left with Alwy.

'They seem a gay bunch,' Waltraud remarked.

'They are not serious officers,' Youssef replied in his stilted manner. 'They have nothing on their minds but drink and women. Don't ever lend them money, Rusty,' he added as an afterthought. 'You won't see it again.'

'Good old Youssef! Don't worry, I'll watch out. But don't you think it was nice of Omar to offer me accommodation for my horses?'

'Yes, it's a good enough solution for the time being, but what you need is a farm. I shall make some enquiries for you.'

'Perfect. And perhaps you'd keep your eyes open for a nice villa too. Now that I'm a respectably married man I need one.'

Youssef, Danny and Nadia all volunteered enthusiastically to help us find a perfect new home, and after another half-hour of coffee and society gossip we all got up to leave. Gerhard Bauch walked us to the car, talking volubly about the bad treatment his horse was getting at the club. He exaggerated a great deal and I wondered what he was after. Finally he came to the point.

'I heard Colonel Hadary offering you stabling facilities

in Abassia. Do you think you could put in a word for me too?'

So that was it! I almost laughed out loud.

'That may be tricky, Gerhard,' I replied casually, 'Hadary would think I was overdoing it a little. You know how touchy they are here. I'm sure you understand.'

With that we waved goodbye and drove off, well pleased with the morning's catch.

'It's just like fishing,' I said to Waltraud, who had hardly been able to contain her amazement. 'You bait the hook, cast the line and wait. If you are lucky you land a big one. As Frederick the Great once said about his generals: "Good fortune is more important than good generalship." Now let's hope our luck holds for this afternoon's races.'

4

The Glorious Past

A good many cars were already parked outside the Von
Leers' residence when Waltraud and I arrived the next evening. The doorman of the two-storey villa directed us to a
parking place nearby.

'Your name, sir?' he asked me in English, consulting a
list.

Being checked in at the gate in this manner when paying a visit to a private person was by no means customary
procedure. Not usual either was the sub-machine gun the
man wore underneath his flowing white galabeyah. The
Mabahes el-Amma – the secret police – were obviously
guardingVon Leers well. We were shown into the house by
another servant, apparently the real article and not a dis-
guised policeman.

Mr and Mrs Von Leers greeted us at the door. He was a
wizened infirm old man with sparse white hair and watery,
pale blue, expressionless eyes. 'Come in, my dear Lotz, come
in. Heil Hitler,' he said in his shaky voice. His wife, somewhat younger and a typical product of the Prussian middle
class, gushed at Waltraud, who was rather taken aback by
this form of salutation.

'And this charming young lady must be Frau Lotz! Do

come in, my dear, we are delighted to make your acquaintance.' Raising her hand to my lips, as I knew was required
of me, I mouthed some obligatory phrases and we were
ushered into the spacious living-room, where at least thirty
people were already assembled, standing or sitting together
in small groups, sipping cocktails and conversing in German, English or Arabic.

'You will meet quite a few old friends here tonight,' said
Mrs Von Leers. 'In a minute I shall introduce those you
don't already know. But first tell me: How was your trip?
How is Germany? It must have changed so much.'

'It was a marvellous trip,' I said. 'But I'm glad to be back.
I like it here.'

'Oh, of course, of course, so do we. We adore Egypt.
It's only that Johann gets so terribly homesick sometimes. If
we could just go for a visit, only for a short visit, you
understand, just once!'

'The professor would be taking quite a risk if he did
that.'

'Yes, yes, it's out of the question! The Jews would throw
him into prison.'

'The Jews?'

'But of course! Germany is dominated by the Jews again.
Nobody else would want to hurt a harmless old man like
my husband. Mr Lotz, aren't you taking rather a risk yourself travelling to Germany so frequently?'

'A risk? In what way?'

'Oh, I just thought... well, never mind. You know, we
had the most exciting visitor the other day! I swore not to
tell who it was. He arrived in great secrecy. Came from
South America. He and Johann spent two whole nights talking. Oh my God, it was like the old days!'

'I heard a rumour that Reichsleiter Bormann was here
for a few days.'

'You said that, I didn't. I promised not to say anything
and I am not telling you who our visitor was. Anyway, I

am talking too much. Come and meet some people.' Waltraud
was standing a few paces away listening to Von Leers.

'. . . and now my name is Omar Amin,' he was saying.

'Stop talking nonsense, dear,' said his wife. 'Your name is
Johann Von Leers and there was no reason to change it.
It is a good and honourable name and one day the German
nation will be proud of you again.'

A tall grey-haired man with a deeply lined face walked in
and came over to us.

'My respects, gnädige Frau, Herr Professor.'

'Heil Hitler, my dear doctor,' exclaimed our host.

'I think "good evening" will do under the circumstances'
grunted the newcomer, glancing around the room.

'Ach, don't mind my husband, he loves to re-live the
past. Let me introduce you to a charming couple: Doctor
Eisele – Mr and Mrs Lotz. Dr Eisele is the official physician
for the aircraft factories. He looks after the German
experts.'

So this was the notorious Dr Eisele. I heard Waltraud
draw in her breath. This man was wanted for mass murder
by the police of at least a dozen countries. As a physician
at Nazi concentration camps he had conducted lethal 'scien-
tific experiments' on inmates, slowly and painfully killing
thousands of men, women and even children. I had heard he
was here, and that the United Arab Republic had given him
political asylum and a well-paid position, but this was the
first time I had met him in person. I shot Waltraud a warn-
ing look, a little afraid of what her reaction might be and
hoping she would take her cue from me. We had to play
our role and this was part of it. Shaking hands with the
fellow and exchanging at least a few words of polite conversation could hardly be avoided unless we wanted to
provoke an unpleasant scene with the eyes of the whole
room on us. I took his extended hand briefly and said I was
pleased to meet him. Waltraud had taken out a handkerchief and was dabbing at her eye. She nodded curtly at

Eisele. 'Excuse me, I have something in my eye. Mrs
Von Leers, would you be so kind as to show me to the bathroom?'

'But of course, my dear,' said the old lady solicitously.
'Come along!' Very neatly done, I thought.

I could fully understand my wife's aversion to shaking
hands with this mass murderer. He made my skin creep too.
On the other hand some of the German experts now in
Egypt were actively engaged in constructing bacteriological
warheads with plague and cholera germs for the Egyptian's
do-it-yourself rockets, and they had to be stopped

An Egyptian whom Von Leers introduced as Dr Ahmed
Something-or-other joined us and began a discussion with
Eisele regarding some new X-ray equipment. Von Leers
took my arm and drew me aside.

'Come, my dear Lotz, let us sit on the verandah for a
while in the fresh air and have a glass of wine. Would you
believe it, I have got a bottle of real Moselle!'

He called a servant and, speaking very slowly in the
classical Arabic of scholars, instructed him to bring the
required bottle. We seated ourselves on wicker armchairs in
the corner of the verandah. The heat of the day had passed
giving way to a cool breeze. Von Leers offered me a cigar
and lit it for me. He himself did not smoke. The servant
brought a bottle and glasses and Von Leers poured the
wine.

'Prosit, my dear boy.'

'Your health, professor.'

'Ah, what a fine wine. You can taste the sun of Southern
Germany.'

'Yes, excellent. And how pleasant it is out here.'

'We are lucky to have a breeze, it drives away the mos-
quitoes.' He took another sip. 'Have you met Dr Eisele
before?'

'No. He doesn't seem to move around much in Cairo
social circles.'

'I mean, didn't you meet him in Germany at some time during the war?'

'No, I never met him. Germany is a big place, professor.'

'Quite. And it used to be much bigger in the great days. I thought perhaps you had come across him during the war. Where exactly did you serve?

'I was in the Afrika Korps, 115th division, as I think I've already told you.'

'Yes, I know you told me. And I quite appreciate your reasons for telling this story to everybody. It's the sensible thing to do. It would be extremely stupid to tell them the truth. Might be dangerous too.'

'I don't understand you, professor? It *is* the truth.'

'Come now, Lotz. You are clever. But you don't have to play this game with me. Am I not to be trusted? The Führer trusted me, Goebbels trusted me, and I have never betrayed them.'

'I really don't know what you are talking about. Nobody questions your trustworthiness, professor, but what has it got to do with the subject we are discussing?'

He smiled knowingly. 'All right, if you don't want to put your cards on the table you don't have to, my dear Obersturmbannführer. I shall certainly not be the one to give you away.'

'Obersturmbannführer? Give me away? What is this, a joke?' I was simply puzzled.

'No joke. Look Lotz, do me the courtesy not to consider me an imbecile! I may be an old man, and some people are saying behind my back that I'm getting slightly senile. But I've always had an excellent memory for faces. I happen to remember yours very well. We met only once, at some conference in Wannsee. I can't recall the exact occasion or the date, but it was during the latter part of the war. I remember you distinctly, looking very smart in the black uniform of an Obersturmbannführer [a Lieutenant-Colonel in the SS]. Don't deny it, my dear boy, I am happy you are one of us and I will keep your secret. None but a chosen few shall know about it, I promise you.'

'A chosen few, professor, you are making a mistake! You are confusing me with somebody else and you must not tell this cock-and-bull story to anyone. Do you want to ruin me? Don't you realize how much harm this can cause me, not here perhaps, but certainly in Germany.'

I was angry now – as well as relieved. But gradually amusement became predominant. I was keeping repellant enough company without having to become part of it. Yet – something was shaping in the back of my mind.

'All right,' he said indulgently, 'I can understand why you don't want these facts to be known. You are luckier than I am, still being able to visit Germany. I'm not going to be the one to spoil all this for you.'

Waltraud came out on to the terrace accompanied by Colonel Mohsen Sabri. Sabri drew me aside and asked me how I'd enjoyed the afternoon's races.

'Very much,' I answered – 'How did you get on? Win, as usual?'

'No, I lost my shirt. In fact I'm absolutely broke. I say, Rusty, do you think you could manage another small loan? I need the money for essential things and I need it urgently. You would be doing me a great favour.'

So it was to be another 'loan'. There had been three or four of those already. The subject of returning the money had of course never come up. Rich foreigners were legitimate game for the likes of him; but refusing would definitely not have been to my advantage.

'How much do you need, Mohsen? Will fifty pounds do?'

'Could you make it seventy-five? And please, Rusty, in dollars, if possible, not Egyptian pounds. I can get more for them.'

It can't be helped, I thought, taking out my wallet, the Israeli taxpayer will have to foot the bill again.

Gathering up Waltraud I led her to the rear of the long

L-shaped room, where a noisy and cheerful group – which included the German experts Brenner and Schonmann – had assembled near the piano. On it stood several bottles of brandy, vodka and Steinhager. Brenner, his bloated face redder than ever, was waving a glass in Schonmann's face.

'And I'm telling you the last test was a success!' he shouted. 'There's nothing wrong with the blades, nothing whatsoever. If it wasn't for the way you geniuses make a mess of anything you touch, we would have it up in the air and in serial production in six months time. Because of your lot it's still in the experimental stage.'

This conversation, I thought, had the makings of a first class and revealing row.

Throwing his head back Brenner emptied his glass and then refilled it. Schonmann took a small sip from his Steinhager and brushed a fragment of cigarette ash off his sleeve. 'It's easy for you to talk, Brenner,' he purred quietly in his melodious Austrian dialect, 'and still easier always to put the blame on others. You know just as well as I do where the fault lies. It's local labour, local so-called engineers, the delay in shipment of parts and a million other things. On top of all that you have the authorities tying us up in red tape. It takes weeks or months just to . . .'

'Don't give me that!' interrupted Brenner. 'In my plant everybody is strictly on the ball. Strictly on the ball at all times. Why don't you come over and visit us some time? You might see a few things worth imitating.'

'Having a family quarrel, gentlemen?' I broke in sweetly. 'I should have thought eight hours a day at the plant would be enough time to talk shop. Gentlemen, I want you to meet my wife.'

They all turned their heads at us, smiling. Those who were seated hurriedly got to their feet.

'Ah the new Mrs Lotz,' cried Brenner. 'This is indeed a pleasure, gnädige Frau. I must admit our horseman here has damn good taste.'

E

'Please be seated, Madame,' said Schonmann after they
all had been introduced, drawing up a chair. 'May I get you
a drink?'

'No more champagne,' said Waltraud taking her seat. 'Perhaps a small whisky with plenty of soda.'

'Right away. What about you, Lotz?'

'I know what his poison is,' laughed Brenner. He filled a
glass with Steinhäger and offered it to me. 'Drink it down,
my boy,' he said a trifle unsteadily, 'you have a lot of catch-
ing up to do.'

'Prosit,' I toasted them. 'Here's to your nuts and bolts or
whatever it is you fellows are playing with all day long.
Apparently at night also. I hope we didn't interrupt a production conference of some sort.'

'To hell with that, begging your pardon, gnädige Frau,'
said Brenner. 'I don't believe in conferences, they're just a
lot of blah. In my plant I give the orders and they are obeyed
without anyone holding conferences and talking rubbish.
Anybody gets out of line, I tear him apart. It's the only way.
That's the trouble with your crowd, Schonmann: no disci-
pline. They are too soft and so are you. Before I take anybody on I have a good look at his war record. Tells you
all about a man. The old hands from the Luftwaffe are the
best. Ex-pilots, flight engineers, some of them used to fly
with the Wilde Sau – the suicide squadron – at the end of the
war. Those boys were wonderful. Remember their squadron
song? Ta-ra-ra ram-ta-ta . . .' He downed another glass, then
seated himself at the piano and struck a chord. 'Remember
the words, horseman? Come on, let's sing!'

Together we sang and some of the others joined in:

> 'Und wenn es bummst und kracht,
> dann weisst Du es genau,
> das war ein Flugzeugführer von der Wilden Sau!'

Von Leers came over, beaming and nodding his head in
time with the song. 'I can see the party is getting under way,'

he said in his shaky old-man's voice. 'Mr Brenner is always the
life and soul. I hope you're enjoying yourself, Mr Lotz, this
reminds one so much of the old days, when young people
were ready to fight for an ideal and had loyalty in their
hearts. Today's youth is only interested in transistor radios
and degenerate American music. When I remember our
clean-cut German boys and girls in their smart uniforms
marching to the tunes of real music ... come, let us have
some of these beautiful old songs, Mr Brenner, and we
shall all sing together. Perhaps "Wir wollen weiter mar-
schieren" or "Unsere Fahne flattert uns voran". I'm sure
Lotz here still remembers all the words,' he added with a
conspiratorial smirk that must have been noticed by everyone up to the far end of the room.

Most of the others gathered round us and the singing
and drinking continued, growing louder and livelier as the
evening went on. We sang the two pieces Von Leers had
requested, and with increased spirit went on to the 'Horst
Wessel Lied' – the stormtroopers' song – 'Als die goldene
Abendsonne' and many others of the same type. I joined in
heartily and carefully with the singing – desperately trying
to remember all the words.

To Von Leers this might have confirmed his belief regarding my personal history, but I could hardly do otherwise as
everyone here knew me for a nationalist German ex-officer
with a great liking for this kind of party. Many of the
Egyptian guests came over to watch and listen with amused
interest. Some of the younger Germans, who had been small
children in the days of the Third Reich, looked somewhat
lost. Waltraud, after an encouraging smile from me, followed
the example of the other German ladies, who had assembled
at a nearby table, making light conversation and observing
us with indulgent fondness.

Brenner was playing the piano well. Not taking the time
to fill his glass between songs, he was now drinking straight
from the bottle. After an hour or so of this entertainment

some of the Germans began showing signs of wear and tear,
wiping their perspiring faces and beginning to look at their
watches. Finally we left.

On the way home Waltraud asked me about my conversation with Von Leers.

'Ah yes, he's found out who I am. Or rather, he thinks
he recognized me.'

'Recognized you! You mean he knows who you are?'

'Oh no, heaven forbid – that would be fatal. Merely a
case of mistaken identity. Quite amusing really, and it might
even turn out to be a blessing in disguise.' I was deliberately
trying to make light of it all. 'He thinks he remembers my
face from a meeting some twenty years back, and that I
was then an Obersturmbannführer in the SS. I denied it,
of course, but he is firmly convinced of it, the old fool.'

'This is really fantastic. So that's what all the Heil Hitler-
ing was about. But why do you think it could be a blessing
in disguise?'

'Well, for one thing former high-ranking Nazis are very
popular with the Egyptians – the authorities in particular –
and some of the German experts with strong Nazi leanings
are going to welcome me with open arms as one of their
own if this story gets around. And I am quite certain it will.
Von Leers is the biggest gossip in town. Of course I am
not going to pass myself off as a former SS officer. On the
contrary, if anybody asks me point blank I am going to
deny it and stick to my Afrika Korps story. But perhaps I
shall not make my denial any too convincing to certain
people. It depends a little on Von Leers.'

And indeed it did, for contrary to his promise (and as I
anticipated) Von Leers spread the story of my SS past all
over Cairo – and the more I denied it, the more everyone
believed it. Egyptian officers and officials came to attention
when we met, and talked smilingly about my glorious past.
Some of the Germans on the other hand, mostly representatives of German firms in Cairo who were, on the whole,

pretty decent chaps, became markedly cool towards me or even stopped seeing me altogether. Finally I decided to turn the situation to my own advantage, and obtained some documents which clearly confirmed all that Von Leers had been saying. I was really proud of that bit of forgery.

I placed the documents in a large manilla envelope and one morning when Waltraud and I were going out riding I left the envelope on the living-room sideboard. When we returned for lunch the envelope was still on the sideboard, and I called the house-boy to ask what it was doing there. Naturally, he protested that he had no idea, that he was not responsible: and the more he protested, the more I ranted on about his daring to leave my most confidential documents lying around for anyone to pick up. I then made a great show of locking the envelope away in a drawer.

Four days later I opened the drawer. The powder I had sprayed over the envelope had been disturbed and the hair which I had glued to both the envelope and the inside of the drawer had vanished. Doubtless, Egyptian Intelligence had borrowed the papers and photographed them. Now they knew exactly who I was, and how much store they should put on my denials.

5

Rusty Bey

'Easy boy, easy!' I drew in the reins, slowing down to a canter. Doctor, my big chestnut stallion, responded obediently to my command. I turned in the saddle and looked behind me. Waltraud was right on my heels. In these last two years she had become quite a horsewoman, riding and training for several hours each day, with a brave disregard for aching muscles, chafed skin and the occasional dislocated knee or elbow. Her favourite stallion Snowball had died six months earlier and she had now a spirited Anglo-Arab mare which she had trained herself.

'She's made a damn good job of it, too,' I thought, as Waltraud drew up beside me on Isis. We were leaving the desert behind, cantering easily along a sandy path which led through an area of densely cultivated land shaded by tall palm trees. Here, in a secluded part of the Nile Delta some ten miles from Cairo, I had leased a fair-sized farm complete with stables, paddocks, a show-ring and even a racing-track. We raised Arab horses and spent our mornings riding and training them. Apart from being a constant source of pleasure and recreation the farm was a frequent meeting place for many of our Egyptian and German friends. Some of them rode out with us, or received riding instruction; others came just to enjoy the scenery and fresh air.

'Everything all right?' I called to Waltraud who was following me now along the narrow path.

'Perfect,' came the reply, 'the gallop did us all a lot of good.'

We lengthened the reins and let the horses walk abreast of each other. They knew the way and needed no guidance. In Germany it was considered dangerous to ride stallions together with mares, but I'd found that with a little training the Arab stallions behaved themselves perfectly well in female company.

'You know, I never tire of the lovely countryside round here,' Waltraud said.

We were riding stirrup to stirrup at a slow walk and smoking – something else that wasn't done in German riding establishments. Suddenly there was a great roar, not unlike the sound of a jet plane taking off, and my stallion shied slightly. I brought Doctor under control with a word and slight pressure from my legs, looked at my watch and noted the time.

A great advantage of this particular farm was its close proximity to the experimental rocket bases situated near the kilometre 33 signpost, off the Alexandria-Cairo desert road. The rockets were fired off fairly frequently and it was important to record and report the exact times and frequency of the launchings.

'Yes,' I said to Waltraud after a pause, 'I'm glad we took the farm. It was money well spent in more ways than one.'

'It's certainly a marvellous cover,' she said. 'Look at the way they all flock here.'

'Yes, it's almost as though the Egyptian General Staff and the technical boys had nowhere else to discuss their problems.'

That was certainly the case, and it seemed that the more forthcoming we were the more they sought our hospitality.

At first Waltraud had been amazed by the open way in which I went about my business. But as I'd told her, there were various kinds of spies, ranging from the nondescript, grey little man who kept very much in the background, drawing no attention to himself, to extroverts like myself who kept themselves so much in the limelight that no one suspected them for a moment. Thus no one would have dreamed (or so I hoped) that the rich and eccentric German horse breeder Lotz, strutting about the racecourse in the red and green national dress of Bavaria, sporting a six-inch high goat's beard on his hat and pronouncing his views in a loud and determined manner, was anything but what he seemed. And in Egypt, once you were taken for what you seemed you could work wonders. I had, for instance, manoeuvred General Abdel Salaam into giving me an entry permit to certain prohibited areas in the Suez Canal zone simply by saying that the fishing in the Bitter Lakes was so much better than elsewhere. It would never have occurred to him to refuse (and insult) his intimate friend who was the intimate friend of so many powerful people.

'It's funny,' I said to Waltraud, 'the Germans are convinced I can't tell an aircraft engine from a coffee grinder. And the less interest I show in it all, the more they insist on telling me. Look at the balance sheet for the last six months: two missile bases including the experimental one, precise progress reports on aircraft production in both plants, exact personal data on practically all German experts in the war factories, details of naval vessels in the Red Sea as well as of all major troop and armour movements to Sinai, not to mention economic and political information. Not a bad bag, though I say it myself.'

'Carry on like this, Oberstürmbannführer,' replied Waltraud, 'and you'll get a medal.'

There was also the war in the Yemen, for through Abdo and others I had obtained precise and regular information regarding movement of troops, ships, armour and equipment

to the Yemen, where Nasser's armies were fighting pro-
longed and not very successful battles against the Yemenite
tribesmen. By now it was only too clear that he had little
chance of winning the Yemen war, despite continuous bombing and the use of poisonous gas. Naturally it was important
for Israel to know what forces were tied down in the Yemen
and what the morale of the Egyptian troops was like.

'By the way,' Waltraud exclaimed, interrupting my
thoughts, 'have you made any recommendations regarding
Horst Wasser?'

'I have reported on him of course but I've not made any
definite recommendations yet. I think I'll watch him a little
longer. There are one two things about him that still worry
me.'

It was also part of my job to do a little 'bird-dogging' –
in other words, to point out prospective candidates for
recruitment as spies and informers. Naturally I never attempted to do any actual recruiting myself – that would
have been fatal. I simply reported on people I thought suitable, giving an assessment of their character together with
details of their work and the information they might have
access to. The rest was up to the boys. If they considered it
worthwhile they would approach the person in question in
their own way and without my knowing anything about it.

We crossed the asphalt road near the entrance to our farm.

'Don't let Isis rush into the stable yard – hold her back,'
I told Waltraud. 'Ah, here comes Abdullah to take our
horses.'

Waltraud pulled a face: 'Isn't that Bauch over there in
the paddock, giving his usual imitation of the Spanish Riding
School?'

'Poor horse!' I replied. 'I may be a little over-sensitive
where dressage work is concerned but having to watch that
kind of performance quite spoils my day.'

'Well, it was you who agreed to let him stable his horse
here.'

'What could I do? He knows we have plenty of room, and that I let others keep their horses here. How could I refuse him?'

Waltraud and I dismounted, put up the stirrup irons and handed the reins to Abdullah, our head groom. We fed our horses some carrots, patting their necks.

'Did you have a pleasant ride, ya saad el Pasha?' asked the old groom. Ever since I'd raised his salary by five pounds a month, he'd promoted me from 'Bey' to 'Pasha'.

'A great ride, thank you Abdullah. Tell me, has Mr Vogelsang been here this morning?'

'Yes, he's having coffee on the terrace. He says he'll be away for some days and asked if I would exercise his mare. He gave me a very generous bakshish.'

'Good for you, Abdullah,' I replied, slapping him on the shoulder. 'Now lead these two in and rub them down.'

Waltraud and I took off our spurs and went to join Vogelsang, one of the German experts, on the terrace.

'How are you, Harry?' I asked, dropping into a chair beside him. 'Abdullah tells me you're going away.'

'Yes,' he replied. 'Rusty, I'd be terribly grateful if you'd allow your groom to exercise my horse while I'm away.'

'Gladly. Are you off on leave?'

'No such luck. It's that conference in Munich. Brenner and all the others will be going too. It's a top level affair.'

'Better make sure you get a hotel reservation. I hear there's a convention in Munich. Hotels will be pretty booked up.'

'All that's taken care of, thank God. I've got my reservation. In fact the confirmation came through this morning.'

He took a slip of paper out of his pocket and showed it to me. As he did so an idea began to form at the back of my mind and I made a mental note of the hotel and the number of his room.

'By the way, Rusty,' he went on, 'where's a good place to buy a new brief-case? Mine's falling to bits. Besides, it's far too small for the plans and documents I'll have to take with me.'

'Why go to all the expense of buying a new one? I've got a brand new brief-case at home which I hardly ever use. You can borrow mine. I'll have it sent over tomorrow.'

'That's really good of you, Rusty. I'd be terribly grateful.'

So far, so good. The old miser had reacted according to form.

*   *   *

Lunch was waiting when we got back, and I hurried through the meal. In just half an hour I had to transmit details of the rocket launchings we'd observed that morning. I'd recently got a new transmitter, larger and more powerful than the one that had been secreted in my riding boot. This one was hidden inside a special pair of bathroom scales.

My original transmitter had proved too small and had ceased functioning properly after a few months. I'd reported this by letter, using the secret ink I'd been supplied with as an alternative means of communication, and had been told to destroy the faulty machine. This was easier said than done, for although I'd smashed the instrument into tiny pieces with a hammer, I couldn't just throw them into the dustbin – and even throwing them into the Nile, which seemed to me the best solution, posed problems, for foreigners were always closely observed, especially when they went on foot. It was a farcical situation, and in the end Waltraud and I had had to hire a rowing boat and spend a whole day picnicking on the river, just so we could dispose of the equipment along with the remnants of our lunch!

'Ten to two,' I said to Waltraud, smiling to myself as I recalled the incident. 'I'd better go upstairs and get to work.'

My transmitting and receiving was done in our bedroom – generally in the early morning at pre-arranged times.

Waltraud and I had now moved from my flat in Zamalek
to a beautiful and spacious villa in the suburb of Giza. It
was tastefully and expensively furnished in English style,
had a large garden and was surrounded by a high fence with
a thick hedge on the inside ensuring privacy. The master
bedroom was on the second floor and best suited for wireless
communication. Obviously it was the only room in the house
where I could lock myself in without causing comment from
the servants.

As I climbed the stairs the doorbell rang.

'See who it is,' I called to Waltraud, 'I can't be disturbed
now.'

She ran up the stairs after me and looked out through
one of the bedroom windows.

'It's Abdo and Fouad,' she said. 'The gardener is just
opening the gate for them. What shall I do?'

'Go down and give them a drink, of course,' I told her.
'Tell them I'm in the shower and that I'll join them soon.
This won't take long.'

I locked myself in, assembled the set and, at two o'clock
sharp, went on the air. When I'd finished, I stowed away
the transmitting equipment, wetted and combed my hair,
and went down to the living-room where Abdo and
Fouad were sipping whisky and talking to Waltraud.

'What a pleasant surprise,' I exclaimed. 'Don't you people
ever do any work, or is this a holiday?'

'We're celebrating the occasion of your bi-annual shower,'
countered Abdo. 'How nice and clean you look, Rusty.'

'Actually,' put in Fouad, 'we're on our way to Alex. We
just dropped in to see how you both were.'

'Abdo was telling me there's been an aftermath to the
swimming party we had the other night,' Waltraud said.

A couple of nights ago Abdo had visited us with his wife
and their two grown-up children. Shortly before midnight
Schonmann and Vogelsang had dropped in and after a drink
or two suggested we all drove out to Schonmann's villa at

Pyramid Gardens for a swim in his pool and a late supper. It had been a gay and carefree party.

'Did you catch cold?' I asked innocently.

'No, I didn't catch cold,' explained Abdo, 'but the State Security people got me out of bed at six in the morning.'

'You mean Fouad's men?' I asked incredulously.

'No, of course not. From a different branch. Two polite gentlemen in civilian suits who asked me what I'd been doing at Mr Schonmann's house.'

'Well if that isn't the limit! What business is it of theirs? I know Schonmann is well guarded, but you're an army general after all and . . .'

'That's precisely why, Rusty. They drew my attention to the existing regulations which state that no officer of the armed forces may have any social contacts with foreigners, foreign experts in particular, without prior permission of the State Security. It's a strict rule.'

'I thought I'd heard Nasser say that the régime stands for freedom, progress and democracy? If these are the manifestations of it . . .'

'Don't be unjust, Rusty,' Fouad interrupted hastily. 'Of course it's ridiculous to put a man like Abdo on the carpet for having a drink with Schonmann, and I told them so, but you mustn't forget we're at war. We have to protect ourselves, and even if some of the measures we adopt aren't popular, believe me they're necessary.'

'I suppose you're right,' I conceded. 'We had a lot of restrictions in Germany too, during the war. But go on, Abdo, what happened then? What did you tell them?'

'Well, I explained the situation,' he continued. 'I told them we'd met Schonmann and the other experts at your house and that we couldn't very well have left the moment they entered – anymore than we could have excluded ourselves from the party that followed, at least not without being blatantly rude.'

'Did they accept your explanation?'

'Oh yes. They said they appreciated my position at the time, but would I kindly remember the regulations in future and avoid contacts with foreigners.'

'Does that mean you must avoid us too? We're also foreigners, you know.'

He laughed. 'Good God, no! They know all about you, Rusty, and our close friendship. You were cleared years ago.' He winked at me. 'They investigated you quite thoroughly then, believe me. But they know you're in sympathy with the regime and a Jew-hater, and it's also come to their attention that some of the Germans here don't like you for it.'

'Those who don't are welcome to stay away. Have another drink.'

'Just a small one. Then we must be off. What are your plans, Rusty? Let's get together next week.'

'On the nineteenth we're going to Mersa Matrouh to pay an overdue visit to Youssef Ghorab.'

'I'd forgotten he's down there now,' said Fouad. 'Some security job, isn't it?'

'Yes. He's director of security for the Western District and acting governor.'

'What do you know, old Youssef's getting on in the world! Acting governor. That should suit the pompous old ass.'

'Now it's you who're being unjust, Fouad,' I told him. 'I'm sure he's most efficient at his job – which is more than can be said for the last governor.'

'That's why they kicked him out, and promoted him to under-secretary of state at some ministry – I forget which. The biggest fools always get the fattest part of the lamb.'

Abdo chuckled. 'Sour grapes, ya Fouad! Rusty, have you told Fouad that precious story of how you were robbed at Mersa Matrouh?'

'What story's that?' asked Fouad.

'It has to be heard to be believed,' I said. 'Last summer

Waltraud and I went camping at Mersa Matrouh. Youssef
put an olive grove at our disposal, as well as a servant and
guard, though he couldn't understand why we preferred our
tent to the comforts of the Governor's mansion. But there
were others with us, and we couldn't split up the party.
There was Bauch and . . .'

'Ah, Mr Gehlen's bright boy,' put in Fouad.

'Gehlen's bright boy? What do you mean?'

'What, you really didn't know, Rusty? Mr Gerhard Bauch
is no less than the resident agent of German Intelligence.
We've been aware of that for a long while now. He's not
very bright, this countryman of yours, and we're giving him
free rein. It's better than removing him and having someone
else we don't know in his place. Naturally, he's under constant surveillance. But go on, Rusty, tell me your story.'

'Well, we'd been there for about a week, and then one
day, when we came back from the sea, we discovered that
some of our things had been stolen. Nothing very valuable,
a carton of cigarettes, a bathing suit, some underwear, things
like that. In the evening, when we were dining with Ghorab,
I mentioned the theft. You should have seen him! My God,
was he furious. He had everybody arrested within a radius
of a mile and interrogations went on for three days. I tried
to pacify him, telling him that the few stolen articles weren't
worth all the fuss. But he would have none of it. The
robbery was a personal insult. After all, we were his guests.

'Finally, we had to leave and I mentioned that we'd be
staying in Alexandria overnight, though I didn't say where.
Well, we'd hardly arrived in Alexandria and found a hotel
when there was a telephone call for me from police headquarters. The duty officer asked me to report to General
Bishbishy first thing in the morning on a very important
matter.'

'You thought they wanted to arrest you, eh?'

'Well, I couldn't remember committing any major crimes,
but in any case an officer came to the hotel in the morning to

escort me. He didn't know what it was all about, but he did
know that they'd contacted almost every hotel in town to
find me, and that all police patrols in the area had the number of my car as well as descriptions of Waltraud and myself. Now, can you guess what it was all in aid of?'

'They'd found the thief?'

'Exactly! General Bishbishy told me over three cups of
coffee that the thief, the former swimming champion of
Mersa Matrouh, had been apprehended and that my property
would be restored. He mentioned that Youssef Bey had
already spoken to the judge and it was agreed that the man
should get five years.'

'That's the police for you,' said Fouad. 'Imagine putting
the whole police force of Alexandria on the alert for the
sake of a bathing suit and a few cigarettes.'

'It's the principle, my dear boy,' mocked Abdel Salaam.
'Thou shalt not steal from the governor's guests. Not bathing suits, not brassieres . . .'

'That's enough,' said Waltraud modestly. 'You're impossible, Abdo!'

'Wait,' I said, 'it gets even better. While I was with General
Bishbishy an officer came in to ask whether the search for
me could now be called off. It seemed that only the General
himself could countermand the order he had given, regard-
less of whether I had been found or not.'

Abdo was greatly amused, Fouad uncomfortable.

'Please, Rusty, don't repeat this story to anyone in Germany,' he begged me. 'The whole thing is a scandal. This
could never happen in the army.'

Abdo smiled ironically, but did not voice an opinion.
'We have to leave now,' he reminded his friend.

'One for the road, fellows?' I asked them.

'Well, just a short one, Rusty. To toast our good friend
Ghorab!'

*   *   *

As soon as they'd left, I jumped into the car and drove to Rivolis, one of Cairo's most elegant shops. There I bought a beautiful and very expensive brief-case which I despatched to Harry Vogelsang with my compliments.

Later that evening I wrote down and coded a message for transmission the next morning. I gave the time of Vogelsang's arrival in Munich, his hotel and room number, and added that he enjoyed female company in the evenings – a diversion that would incidentally take him out of his hotel room for some length of time. I'd kept the spare key to the brief-case and this I despatched to the boys a couple of days later.

6

Look Over Your Shoulder

It was the spring of 1964, and time for our six-monthly trip to Europe. I had just sold two beautiful thoroughbred Arabian horses, a stallion and a mare, to a horse-crazy Italian millionaire who had visited Egypt. My customer, Baron Enrico di Portanova, had chartered a special transport plane for the horses and invited Waltraud and myself to fly over with them and deliver them personally. In Rome we were the Baron's guests, and each morning, at his special request, we rode and showed the horses off at the magnificent riding track of the Villa Borghese. The nights were spent in noisy champagne parties.

This time, of course, we had the perfect excuse for our trip to Europe, which meant we hadn't had to fall back on Waltraud's illness again – the non-malignant brain tumour we told everyone she had, and for which she needed both the Egyptian sun and periodical treatment in Germany. It was not easy then for a European to get in and out of Egypt at will. Tourist visas were issued for a maximum period of three months and if, when the three months were up, a foreigner wished to remain longer in Egypt, he had to be-come a temporary resident – and a temporary resident had to apply for an exit visa every time he wanted to leave the country, an elaborate and time-consuming business.

Obviously, I hadn't wanted my movements hindered in this way, any more than I'd wanted to draw official attention to my regular trips to Europe. Fortunately, Youssef Ghorab had come to my rescue – after I'd observed that the palaver involved every time I needed to take Waltraud to Germany was getting on my nerves.

'What's the problem?' he'd asked sympathetically. 'We'll give you the status of a permanent tourist. It's a little irregular, but who cares. Just give me your passport every three months and I'll have it stamped and back to you within a few hours.' And that was that.

From Rome we flew to Paris, where I was to meet the boss. Leaving Waltraud in the hotel, I went out into the street to find a phone box. There was one on the corner. I stepped inside, dropped the necessary coins into the slot and dialled a certain number. The phone was answered immediately, and after I'd given the code word I was told to meet a friend at three o'clock in a certain café. In fact, three o'clock at café X meant two o'clock at café Y. One never knew when a conversation was being overheard or tapped and it was vital to take every precaution, to look over your shoulder all the time.

The procedure was this. You arrived at the appointed place at the exact time and waited for precisely three minutes. If either you or your contact failed to appear within those three minutes, you'd meet at another pre-arranged spot exactly an hour later. If you even suspected a tail, you didn't turn up.

I arrived at the rendezvous on time, chose a table at the back of the café and ordered a pernod. Two minutes went by and no one appeared. I began to wonder whether something was up. I recalled with amusement how on my last visit my contact had failed to appear – not because of a sinister shadow but simply because he'd been caught in a traffic jam.

I looked at my watch, and then, out of the corner of my eye, saw my man – an old friend – coming towards me. He greeted me warmly, ordered a drink, drank it slowly, then took me to meet the boss.

Two intensive days of debriefing, briefing and consultation followed. The boss was particularly pleased with my reports on the various rocket bases.

'Incidentally,' he told me, 'we got a good aerial photograph of that dummy military airport near the Cairo-Alexandria desert road.'

'Dummy?' I replied. 'That's no dummy. Those planes are all too real.'

'But that's impossible,' he exclaimed. 'Why would the Egyptians parade scores of aircraft along the tarmac, in two straight lines, unless they wanted us to notice them. They *must* be dummies.'

'I assure you they're not,' I replied vehemently. 'One of my good friends from the airforce was kind enough to invite me to inspect them only a few weeks ago. I was within a few feet of them. Take my word for it. They're real.'

The boss laughed. 'Well, I suppose anything's possible in Egypt. Haven't they heard of dispersal? By the way,' he added, becoming serious again, 'I have some other photographs here which I don't like. Tell me, Wolfie, have you gone completely out of your mind?'

He threw down on to the table a copy of the German riding magazine, *Reiter Revue*, and pointed to one of the pages. There were several photographs of me on horseback, including one in which I posed proudly with one of my horses after a win.

'How on earth do you come to allow a magazine to photograph you in this way? It only needs one talkative person in Israel to recognize you and the game's up.'

He was absolutely right, of course, but I could hardly

have prevented those pictures from being published. The head of the German Horsebreeders' Association had visited Cairo recently, and since I was an esteemed member of the same association I had naturally spent some time with him. He had taken a few snaps of me on horseback but never mentioned he was a regular contributor to the *Reiter Revue*.

I explained the matter to the boss as best I could. Then, when he was pacified, I submitted my bi-annual financial report, which he signed after a cursory glance.

'You'll want more money, I suppose,' he said, 'I'll make the transfer to your German bank account in the usual way. Wolfie, my "dear friend",' he added with a chuckle, 'they say a top agent is worth a brigade. You're making me painfully aware of the fact he also costs as much.... Well, I suppose we have to keep your generals happy,' he added as an afterthought.

We now came to the briefing session. The boss was particularly anxious for me to get details about the assistants that were being recruited in Germany by Karl Knupfer, the new head of the rocket guidance programme.

'When are you going back?' he asked. 'It's very urgent.'

'In about three weeks,' I replied. 'Waltraud and I need a little leave and relaxation – and I also have to go shopping for my Egyptian friends. But if it's that urgent I suppose we could fly back.'

'No, don't do that,' he exclaimed. 'I've told you before, spies fly and decent people go by ship – so you must go by ship.'

As we parted he told me an amusing story. It was proving hard to get people into Egypt for any length of time, and one of our agents there had been asked to suggest a good cover. He had replied: 'Why not buy a horse farm there like that Nazi bastard Lotz. All the high-ranking Egyptian officers and officials flock to his bloody farm. They're mad about him.' – 'Oh no,' the boss had replied coolly. 'Who wants to get involved with horses. We have enough trouble with the Egyptians!'

*   *   *

Three weeks later, Waltraud and I sailed from Trieste on the *Ausonia*. After just a few hours we docked at Venice. I stood by the rail, enjoying the sun and watching the passengers as they slowly mounted the gangway. I knew quite a few of them, mostly Germans returning from their annual holiday, but two men I'd never seen before caught my eye. They'd appeared in two big Mercedes cars and certainly didn't look like tourists. One had a wife and three children with him; the other was alone.

That evening I saw one of the men drinking alone in the bar. I climbed on to the stool beside him, and we soon got talking. I asked him if this was his first trip to Egypt and he replied in the affirmative.

'I suppose you're a tourist,' I began.

'Oh no. I'll be working in Egypt for the next six years.'

'Where?'

'Oh, I really don't know.'

The Egyptians always tried to impress on their new German advisers the need for secrecy, and so I was immediately suspicious.

'You mean to say you're going to work in Egypt for six years and you don't know where?' I asked incredulously, pressing him a little.

'Well, not exactly,' he explained hastily. 'You see it's a government job so I really won't know the exact details until I get there. I'll be met at the port by one of my colleagues.'

I gave him my card, saying I hoped to see more of him in Cairo. He could do no less than hand me his in return. On it was printed: 'Erich Traum, Electronic Engineer'.

The following morning a number of passengers were lazing around the swimming pool on the upper deck, listening to a transistor radio. It was a particularly expensive machine, and they were discussing its various merits. I turned to Traum, who was reading in a deckchair, and asked for his professional opinion.

'Why ask me,' he exclaimed, 'I know nothing about such matters.' Suspicion was written all over him.

'Well, you're an electronic engineer,' I answered. 'It says so on your card.'

'Yes, of course it does,' he stammered. 'But how do you know I deal with things like radios and radar?'

'I just thought you might,' I replied, and changed the subject.

*   *   *

A few days after our return to Cairo, Waltraud and I went to the Knupfers' for tea. Ever since Knupfer had arrived to take charge of the rocket programme, we'd been trying to strike up a friendship with him and his wife.

Mrs Knupfer happened to notice my gold monogrammed cufflinks and drew me aside to ask where I'd got them. It was her husband's birthday next week, she explained, and she'd love to buy him a similar pair. I told her I'd had mine made at a small shop in the Mousky bazaar, in the old city of Cairo. Since it was an impossible place to find, I gallantly offered to take her there.

I called for her in my car at four o'clock the following afternoon. On the way into town she asked me all about our trip to Germany – what the weather had been like, what we had done, and so on.

'One of the things I enjoyed most,' I told her, 'was the boat trip back. Incidentally,' I went on, 'I met a couple of your husband's colleagues on board.'

'Oh,' she exclaimed, 'you mean Traum and Ebehard. They live down the road from us, in Nasser city. They're to be Karl's senior assistants.'

And she promptly proceeded to tell me all about them.

7
Rockets and Champagne

I had just finished a lengthy transmission, and as I put down the headset and switched off the wireless receiver, Waltraud called sleepily from the bed:

'Have you finished?'

'Almost,' I replied, 'I got the message all right. Reception was nice and clear today. I'll be through with de-coding in about fifteen minutes. This is a long one. Go back to sleep for a while.'

Wearily I picked up notebook, cipher key and pencil and went to work.

I looked at the sheet of paper I had used for writing, read the message again, memorized it, then stepped into the adjoining bathroom where I burned it and flushed the ashes down the toilet.

Waltraud sat up in bed when she heard me returning. 'Is it anything important, dear?' she asked.

'Yes, I'm afraid it is,' I replied. 'Very important and most urgent. Top priority in fact. It's about that rocket base in Shaloufa again.'

We had recently spent a good deal of time looking for the concealed rocket base. Headquarters knew all about it from aerial photographs. They had, however, a sneaking suspicion that it might be a dummy and therefore it was vital for me to verify it at all costs and by any means I thought suitable.

'The base is between Suez and Ismailia,' I told Waltraud. 'I shall have to go and see the damn thing for myself. It's the only way to verify it.'

'May I come too?'

'Of course, partner. We'll take some rods and disguise the whole thing as a fishing trip.'

'You know, I rather like it when you call me partner.'

'Well, isn't that what you are? You know that for me a wife must be more than a housekeeper or bed companion. She must share everything. That's why my first two marriages went on the rocks.'

'Well, you know you can count on me. Now where exactly shall we look? We've already scanned the area twice.'

From a drawer I took out some maps, selecting one of the Canal area south of Suez. I unfolded the map on my knee.

'Now let's try and work this out by elimination,' I said. 'This is the desert road running roughly north-south between Ismailia and Suez. Here is the railway line running parallel to the road. At some places they are close together, at others some distance apart. Now, the place we are looking for is supposed to be between the railway line and the road, right?'

'Yes, but we drove all along that road and back and after that you even went by train to get a view from the other side and neither of us saw anything resembling a rocket base.'

'Correct. So we can safely eliminate all those areas where the road can be seen from the railway or the other way round. You can't hide a rocket base in a mud hut or under a palm tree. It has to be an area of some size. There are three such places,' I said, pointing with my finger, 'up here, here, and there a little further down. Another thing: there has to be some sort of road leading to it.'

'I remember two roads branching off the desert highway,'

said Waltraud. 'One is just a track leading to a garbage
dump or something, and the other is guarded by a soldier
and has a sign "No entrance and no photography." '

'Well, there are a million places like that all over Egypt,
especially in the Canal Zone.'

But I remembered the place. We hadn't gone in because
of the guard and also because I thought we might have been
able to see the place from some other observation point.
But we hadn't. As a result I decided to drive down there
with Waltraud that morning, posing as ordinary tourists
out for a swim in the Bitter Lakes.

Dressed in slacks, a yellow sports shirt with blue spots
and a bright red peaked cap, I set off with Waltraud to do
a little spying.

                    *   *   *

Suez was less than an hour's drive from Heliopolis. Just
before reaching the unsightly town itself, we turned left,
crossed the railway lines and went on to the desert road
leading to Ismailia. Traffic was light.

Eventually I stopped the car on a lonely stretch of road
to consult my map.

'Why don't I take the wheel for a bit,' said Waltraud,
'so you can take your eyes off the road and observe better.'

'Good idea.' We changed places and while she did the
driving I traced our progress on the map. We passed some
mud dwellings and a military camp and after that there was
nothing but desert again. 'Slow down a little,' I said after
we had gone on at a fast pace for some ten kilometres, 'we
are almost there. Here is the track to the garbage dump.
Our intersection is only two or three kilometres ahead.'

'Can we cut through the desert from here?' asked
Waltraud.

'I'm looking for a suitable spot to turn off the road,' I
replied, 'but it looks pretty hopeless. All deep sand – we'd

get stuck in no time. Let's see what it's like a little further on.'

Try as we might, we couldn't find a stretch of desert which was firm enough to drive across. Very soon the road leading to our destination came into view, branching off to the right. There was no barrier, but a sentry box stood near the crossing.

'What do I do now?' Waltraud inquired. 'Do I go straight in?'

'No, stay on the main road,' I said, 'change into low gear and drive on slowly. I want to see what kind of a guard they have and if there is more than one.'

There was only one soldier with a military police armband leaning idly against the side of the sentry box. A revolver hung from his side in a webbing holster that had once been white. He paid no attention to us as we drove past on the main road. As soon as we were out of sight behind one of the many low hills we stopped.

'Let's turn back,' I said, 'and try again. We shall have to get in somehow. We may have to stage a breakdown and ask for help – or something of the sort.'

Waltraud made a U-turn and we went back in the opposite direction.

'Stop near the intersection and we'll have our breakdown,' I instructed her, 'we'll get out of the car and start fiddling with the engine.'

We came to a halt directly opposite the sentry box.

'Wait, don't get out,' I exclaimed, 'this is too beautiful to be true!'

The scene which met our eyes would not, perhaps, normally be described as beautiful, but at that moment it had a definite attraction for me. The soldier's belt and revolver holster were hanging from a nail on the side of his little hut. The soldier himself had withdrawn some twenty or thirty yards into the desert, where he was squatting in the sand relieving himself, his trousers dropped to the ground.

'In, quickly!' I shouted. 'Drive as fast as you can!' Waltraud slammed into gear and, spinning the steering wheel sharply to the left, took off like greased lightning. As we sped past the sentry box and a black and red signboard reading 'prohibited area' in Arabic and English, I heard a faint cry from behind us. I looked in the driving mirror, turning it slightly, and saw the sentry stumbling to his feet, his trousers held up with one hand, his other hand waving frantically. 'Don't turn your head,' I said, 'and keep going. Somebody may try and stop us at any minute and I want to get a look at that base first.'

I was literally making a forced entry into a top secret area – in broad daylight, wearing a flowered shirt, and accompanied by my wife in a speeding car. Gradually the road dropped into a valley and our soldier was no longer to be seen. A turn, a rise, another valley. 'Somebody's coming,' said Waltraud. A jeep full of soldiers was approaching from the opposite direction.

'Keep going,' I urged, 'unless they stop us.' The jeep went by, the five soldiers in it staring at us curiously.

'Take it easy now,' I said to Waltraud, 'let's find a vantage point from where we can see the base.' I glanced into the driving mirror. 'Ah-ha, the fun is starting. They've turned around and are following us.'

'What happens now,' she asked shakily, 'should I accelerate and try to lose them?'

'No point in that. It would look suspicious. Let them overtake us. But we have to prevent them from kicking us out of here before we know exactly what they keep here. They may just give us a lecture and make us drive straight back.' Then I suddenly had an idea. 'Tell you what: drive the car right into the sand! If you can get us really stuck, we may have to stay here for hours. Quick, off the road – and make it convincing!'

Waltraud increased her speed and began swerving from one side of the road to the other. 'Anything for a bit of fun!' she said between her teeth. 'Hold on to something, here she goes!'

Disregarding a bend she went straight on and landed us with a bump in the deep sand beyond the shoulder of the road.

'Keep the wheels turning,' I told her, 'it will dig us in deeper.'

'Poor little car.' She put her into first gear and raced the motor.

'Never mind the car. What we're after here is worth a thousand cars. That's enough, they are coming. Out now, and I'll start shouting at you.'

'At me?'

'Sure. Let's give them their money's worth. The stupid wife of the stupid tourist being cursed for driving in such an infernally stupid manner.'

Screaming at her and gesticulating wildly I did my best to give a convincing imitation of an infuriated husband. The jeep stopped near us, and the five soldiers, armed with sub-machine guns, jumped down and surrounded us. The Sergeant in charge addressed me in Arabic:

'What are you doing in this area? How did you get here?'

I replied in English: 'Nice of you to come and help. Come on, give me a hand!'

'Mish fahim – I don't understand. What are you doing here?'

'Do you speak English? Deutsch?'

He shook his head. 'Mish fahim.'

I opened the boot of the car and took out a small spade I always carried with me. 'Are you going to help me dig out this car?' I asked in German, gesturing with my hands to make my meaning clear. The Sergeant, in turn, motioned to us to get into the jeep. 'You are under arrest,' he said in Arabic. 'I must take you to the guardroom.'

I shrugged my shoulders and began to start digging. 'I

don't know what you are talking about. All right, if you don't want to help, don't.'

The Sergeant aimed his sub-machine gun at my belly and the other soldiers followed his example. Then he pointed the barrel at the vehicle shouting at me: 'Yalla – jeep.' I shook my head and sat down on the fender of the Volkswagen.

'No jeep,' I said. 'I'm not moving from here unless it's in my own car.' He did not, of course, understand my words but their meaning was unmistakable.

'Let's take them by force,' one of the soldiers said.

'Shut up,' the Sergeant told him. 'I'm making the decisions.' He deliberated for some minutes and finally said to the driver: 'Go over to the base and report to the duty officer that we have found two foreigners within the limits of the restricted area with their car stuck in the sand. Tell the officer we cannot talk to them in their language and ask him for instructions. Hurry! Meanwhile we shall stay here and watch them.'

'What were they saying?' asked Waltraud.

'He told me we were under arrest and when I refused to get into the jeep he dispatched the driver to see an officer about it.'

She laughed. 'This is the first time I've ever been arrested.'

'This may not be as funny as you think. They are simple-minded, but they do take their security very seriously. It will be quite a job to talk ourselves out of this. We may have to get Youssef to help us and even so it won't be pleasant. It means exploiting our connections to the utmost. He will pull all kinds of strings if we get into trouble, but there are limits to what he can do, and capers like this are likely to leave an after-taste of suspicion. It can't be helped, though, the main thing is to do what we came for.'

'I think we've already done that. It's obvious this is a secret military installation of some sort.'

'Yes, but we are not positive that it is what we think it is. We shall soon find out though, I hope.' I took out a packet of cigarettes and lit one for Waltraud and one for myself. The rest I offered to the soldiers who accepted them eagerly. One of them approached the car and looked inside.

'They have some nice things here,' he called out to the others. 'A camera and clothes and a carton of American cigarettes. Let's make a search.'

'You keep your hands off their property or we'll all be punished,' snapped the Sergeant. 'If they complain there will be trouble.'

'How can they complain,' retorted the initiator of the scheme, 'they will be in prison.'

We were interrupted by the return of the jeep. Next to the driver sat a Captain in khaki fatigue dress, a revolver on his hip. The soldiers came to attention as he climbed out of the jeep. 'Good morning,' he said unsmilingly in English. 'What is all this about?'

'Well, you can see for yourself, Captain,' I replied. 'We seem to have got stuck in the sand and it will take more than this little spade to get us out again. Do you think you can pull us up to the road with your jeep? I have a tow rope.'

'I'm not concerned about your car at present. What are you doing here? How did you get in here?'

'What do you mean, how did we get in? In our car obviously. We came from Cairo. As to what we are doing here – if it's any of your business – we are on our way to the Bitter Lakes for a swim. Is that a crime? Do you know that these soldiers threatened to shoot us! When I get back to Cairo I shall complain about this at police headquarters where I have many influential friends.'

He was not impressed. 'Are you Americans?' he asked.

'We are Germans and not used to this kind of treatment. We greatly resent it.'

'Why did you come here?'

'I just told you. We are going to the Bitter Lakes.'

'This is not the way to the Bitter Lakes. This is a pro-

hibited area. There is a sign. And how did you get past the
guard?'

'What guard? What sign? As a matter of fact I was asleep.
My wife was driving, that's why we're stuck up to our
ears in the sand now.' I expected him to be amused at this
remark but if he was he did not show it.

'Show me your passports,' he demanded. I handed them
over. He looked at them briefly and put them into his
pocket. 'Here, give those back to me,' I protested. 'They
are the only travel documents we have.'

'They will be returned to you at the proper time. What
have you got in your car?'

'Nothing much. Look for yourself.' He walked over to
the car and looked in.

'Ah, you have a camera! What photographs have you
taken?'

'None yet. I put in a new film only this morning, just
before we left.'

'Why?'

'My God, what questions you ask! Because I want to
take some snapshots of our picnic, the one you are doing
your best to spoil for us. Is that so extraordinary?'

He did not reply but proceeded to search our car in the
most thorough manner. He took the camera from the back
seat and slung it over his shoulder. Then he discovered the
road map in the side pocket of the door, inspected it and
stuck it into his belt. He looked under the seats, opened the
boot and even the bonnet, but apparently found nothing else
he deemed important.

'Have you any firearms?' he asked.

'No, we are not on safari,' I replied impatiently. 'Why
should I have firearms? Look, Captain, aren't you overdoing
this a little? What do you want from us? If this is the way
you treat well-paying tourists in your country not many
will come here, I assure you. What is this inquisition all
about?'

'You will have to come with me.'

'Come with you? Where?'

'To the ... to my camp. It is not far. The Colonel will want to see you.'

'I suppose we might as well come with you. It will give us the chance to speak to your superior. He may show more sense. But what about our car?'

'It will remain here under guard. It's evidence.'

I locked the Volkswagen carefully and helped Waltraud into the jeep, beside the driver. The Captain ushered me into the back. He ordered the soldiers to guard our car and not to touch anything and we drove off in the direction Waltraud and I had been heading for. After a few hundred yards we went through a road block manned by two military policemen, then up a steep hill, and there it was right below us. There could be no mistake – the rocket launching sites arranged in a wide circle, the storage bunkers, the administration buildings at some distance from the other installations. This was it all right. Waltraud had the sense not to turn round, but I saw the back of her neck going red with excitement.

We drew up before a heavy iron gate which was opened at a sign from the Captain, who then directed the driver to what appeared to be the main administration building. We were led along a wide passage into the right wing of the building and entered an office where a Sergeant-Major was doing some paper work at a desk. He got up and stood to attention.

'Is the Commandant in?' asked the Captain.

'Yes, effendim. Colonel Fathy is with him.'

'Ask him if he will be kind enough to see me on a matter of the greatest urgency.' The Sergeant-Major went through an adjoining door into the next room and returned after a moment. 'The Commandant will see you, effendim,' he said.

The Captain signalled us to sit down. 'Keep an eye on

G

these two,' he ordered the Sergeant-Major. 'I hold you responsible for them until I return.'

Then he went into the next room, closing the door behind him.

'Don't talk,' I whispered to Waltraud. 'I must try and hear what they are saying.'

I heard the Captain speaking at some length but could make out only odd words like 'foreigners', German passports', 'most suspicious', 'searched the car', 'arrested them'.

Then suddenly I heard another voice raised in anger: 'You mean to say you brought them here?!!! You idiot!! Are you out of your mind?' There was another mumble I could not understand and then the loud voice again: 'At least you could have blindfolded them! You have the sense of a water buffalo. Next thing you will be inviting them to an inspection of the installations. All right, the harm is done now. Bring them in.'

The Captain reappeared, his face crimson. 'Come in,' he barked.

We entered a spacious office, comfortably furnished with leather armchairs, two settees and thick carpets. Behind a huge highly polished desk with four telephones on a side table, one red, one black, and two white, sat the Commandant, a full Colonel. He was about forty years old, very slim, with short-cropped dark hair and a black moustache. On the desk in front of him were our passports, my camera and the road map. To his left, on the edge of a chair, sat a somewhat younger officer in the uniform of a Lieutenant-Colonel. Both men inspected us from head to foot.

'Please sit down,' said the Commandant finally. He picked up one of the passports, then the other, turning the pages slowly. 'You are Mr and Mrs Lotz?' I replied in the affirmative. 'You are Germans. Are you tourists in our country?'

'We live in Cairo.'

'Yes, I can see from your passports that you have been here for some time. What do you do?'

'I am a horsebreeder.' His bushy eyebrows went up.

'A horsebreeder?'

'Yes. What's so strange about that?' I took out my wallet. 'Here is my visiting card with my address in Cairo, this is my identification as a steward of the racing club, and these are membership cards of the Cavalry Club, the Horsemen's Association and the Gezira Sporting Club.' I placed them all on his desk and he inspected the documents one by one.

'If you breed horses in Cairo, Mr Lotz, what are you doing here in a prohibited area?' he asked.

'Now look here, Colonel. I have been through all this with your Captain. He has already conducted an endless and mostly irrelevant investigation of our "crimes". I suggest that, in order to save a lot of questions and answers and misunderstandings, I tell you the whole story. Then every thing will be cleared up.'

'Go on, Mr Lotz. I might as well tell you that you have got yourself into a most unpleasant situation. Breaking into a forbidden military area is a most serious matter.'

'I wouldn't know about that. What actually happened is this: My wife and I came down from Cairo early this morning for a swim and a picnic by the Bitter Lakes. We came on the Suez-Ismailia road. My wife was driving and ...'

'Why was your wife driving? Isn't it more natural for the man to drive?'

'Perhaps. I hurt my knee last week and I wanted to rest it. Besides, my wife enjoys driving.'

'How did you hurt your knee, Mr Lotz?'

'Falling off a horse, getting out of the bath, does it matter?'

'Don't get excited, Mr Lotz, I'm just trying to get the facts.'

'All right, the facts are these: My wife was driving, I fell asleep and she must have taken the wrong turning. I woke up when our car got stuck in the sand. That's all I know. Then your trigger-happy soldiers came along and threatened us. Are you satisfied now, Colonel?'

'Not quite. The sentry at the intersection where our road branches off says he tried to stop you and you went through ignoring his order to stop.'

'I saw no sentry. I'm telling you I was asleep.'

'Your wife was not asleep. Why didn't she stop? There is also a written notice prohibiting entrance to unauthorized persons.'

'My wife saw nothing of the kind. Certainly no one tried to stop her. If your sentry, who was probably sleeping, is telling the truth, why didn't he telephone your office and report the matter?'

'The line to the first road block is out of order, but that is none of your concern. If the man was sleeping he will be punished. As for you and your wife, Mr Lotz, I shall inform the proper authorities and a full investigation will be made.'

'But this is ridiculous, Colonel. My wife and I were looking forward to a nice outing and a swim. Why on earth should we want to come here instead, to look at a military barracks in a particularly unattractive piece of desert? Tell me that!'

'You may be spies or saboteurs for all I know. The authorities will look into it.'

'This is preposterous.' I was beginning to sweat again. 'Really, Colonel, this is going beyond a joke. Let me tell you that I am pretty well known in this country. Why don't you pick up one of your telephones and get through to General of Police Youssef Ghorab. A close personal friend of mine. He will vouch for me. Do you know who he is?'

The Commandant paused. 'Yes, I know who he is, but he has no jurisdiction over us. All the same, a recommendation from him should carry weight with the security people.'

'Security people! Colonel, you have just solved the whole problem. Do you mind if I use your phone?'

'What for?'

'To call some of the security people you have been talking
about. Let's start with General Fouad Osman.'

'You know him?'

'Him and a few others.' I took out a notebook. 'Here is
the number. Call him and he will confirm that I am no spy.
He knows me intimately.'

He opened my passport again and leafed through it, then
threw it back on to the desk. To the Lieutenant-Colonel he
said in Arabic:

'A very strange affair. Do you think he is telling the
truth?'

'Anna aref? How do I know?' replied the other sceptic-
ally. 'It is best not to get involved in this kind of complica-
tion. Why not hand them over to the security police and
let them carry on with the investigation? That's the regular
procedure.'

'If only that fool Adly hadn't brought them into the base.
They won't like that. It will not look well on my record.'

'He claims he is friendly with General Osman. How would
he know people like Osman and Ghorab? Perhaps he is
really one of the German experts.'

The Commandant threw me an uncertain glance. 'Mr
Lotz,' he asked, 'are you sure you are a horsebreeder?'

'I told you so, didn't I?' I retorted angrily. 'But since
you seem to have decided to accept nothing I tell you at
face value, why don't you do as I suggest and have my
statements confirmed by someone whose job it is to deal
with such matters!'

He thought that over for a while, finally arriving at a
decision.

'All right,' he said, lifting the receiver from one of the
telephones at his side, 'I will call General Osman. What was
the number you said?'

I gave it to him and he ordered the call to be put through.
We all waited silently for some minutes. Nearby someone
was shouting at the top of his voice, trying to get a line to

Cairo. I opened a fresh packet of cigarettes and, when the officers declined to smoke, lit one for Waltraud and myself.

A buzzer sounded. The Commandant answered it. 'Yes – What? – Oh, I see. – Ask him to be so kind as to call me back.' Replacing the receiver he addressed me again: 'General Osman is not at his office. It is not known when he will return.'

'That is very unfortunate,' I said, 'but we can get in touch with somebody else. Are you acquainted with Colonel Mohsen Sabri of the state security?'

'No, I've never heard of him. He has nothing to do with us. There are many officers in the different branches of state security.'

'All right, Colonel, let me speak to him and speak to him yourself, and if you are not satisfied he'll refer you to an authority you consider competent. Is that fair enough?' I consulted my notebook. 'This is the number.'

For a moment he seemed undecided then said rather impatiently: 'Very well, I don't see what harm it can do, except that I make a nuisance of myself and bother a lot of people who have more important things to do.' In an angry voice he gave Sabri's number to the operator.

The operator must still have had the line open, because the call came through almost immediately.

'Hello . . . Who is that speaking? . . . The adjutant? . . . This is Colonel Abdel Aziz Mohsen, may I speak to Colonel . . . eh . . . Sabri please . . . Hello . . . Colonel Sabri? Good morning to you. Excuse the question, Colonel, but would you be good enough to tell me what branch of the service your office belongs to . . . I see . . . I see . . . Oh yes. I will tell you why I'm asking this. I have a rather strange situation on my hands here. Are you by any chance acquainted with a German couple called Lotz? You are! You know them well? . . . What? . . . Who are they? . . . Because they are sitting right here in my office under arr . . . well, I mean I have had to detain them here temporarily. They drove into my installa-

tion this morning as if it belonged to them. I don't have to
tell you what that means... What?... Yes Colonel, of
course there is a guard on the base... Yes, outside too...
No, no, of course not. We are not at fault. Perhaps one of my
junior officers was a little rash and brought them inside. No,
they were not in the base, they were in the vicinity, in the
prohibited area... Yes, I know I said that, but... no, I suggest we discuss this some other time. We are not to blame,
I assure you. The point is, I mean my question to you is
what to do with these Germans... Yes, certainly.' He handed the instrument to me, his face a shade paler than before.
'Colonel Sabri wishes to speak to you.' I put the receiver to
my ear. 'Hello, Mohsen!' His voice at the other end was
faint but clear: 'Good morning, Mr Lotz! What's this
trouble you've got yourself into? What are you doing in a
secret installation of the armed forces?' His voice had a
slight edge to it. Was he suspicious?

'I'll tell you, Mohsen. We are here, my wife and I, because we were forcibly taken into this place by an armed
escort. We were driving to the Bitter Lakes for a picnic. We
took a wrong turning off the main road, it seems, and got
stuck in the sand with our car. Then some soldiers came and
handled us very roughly. Their officer, a Captain, does not
know how to behave himself either and, after confiscating
our property, forced us, practically at gunpoint, to come to
these blasted barracks. Now we are being interrogated like a
couple of criminals and they don't believe a word we say.
I called Fouad and he wasn't in. When I get back to Cairo
some people are going to hear of the hospitable treatment
they afforded us. I am sorry to bother you, Mohsen...'

'No bother at all,' he interrupted me. His voice was more
affable. 'I'm glad you called me about this. I'm sure there
has been some misunderstanding. The fact remains that you
entered a forbidden area. They might have accepted your
explanation, but these men are a little touchy and excitable.
The orders are very strict. We are on a war footing and

can't take any chances, you must understand that. Anyone entering this area is to be arrested. Of course, in your case I shall see that you are cleared at once. I will also talk to Fouad, in case a report is submitted. Now, give me that Colonel again, please. My regards to Mrs Lotz and apologies for the inconvenience. I'll see both of you in Cairo. Goodbye for now.'

'Goodbye, Mohsen, and thank you. Oh, by the way, can you ask them to help us with our car? ... O.K. fine.'

I pushed the instrument across to the Commandant who listened attentively to what Sabri was saying to him. His own contribution to the conversation consisted of monosyllabic replies of 'yes' and 'of course'. I heard cackling noises coming from the earpiece, but could not understand what was being said at the other end. The Commandant's face was a study in discomfort and embarrassment.

Once more the power that the security services wielded in Egypt was being demonstrated to me. Here was a Colonel, Commandant of an important secret missile base, who had done nothing but act according to orders, actually cringing in the most servile manner before an officer of equal rank who was in no way entitled to give him instructions of any kind. But that particular officer belonged to a branch of the secret service and could, if he wished, make life exceedingly uncomfortable for those who offended him.

'Naam, effendim, Khader effendim,' he was saying now, 'as you order. I shall attend to it immediately. The matter will be settled to your complete satisfaction. Yes, I understand ... forgive me, I had no way of knowing ... yes, certainly. Goodbye effendim, thank you.'

He threw the receiver on to the hook and nervously rose to his feet, at the same time creasing his features into the semblance of what he obviously considered to be an engaging smile. 'My apologies, Mr and Mrs Lotz. Colonel Sabri has explained the situation to me. I very much regret this misunderstanding, but you must realize that we have our orders. National defence secrets must be carefully protected and no unauthorized persons allowed near the sites where they are installed. It is quite clear to me now that you meant no harm – indeed, a man of your status – and that you were the victim of – a navigational error made by Madame. It could have happened to anyone. The sentry should have stopped you, but apparently he neglected his duty. He will be very severely punished.'

'There is nothing to apologize for, Colonel,' I said magnanimously. 'You acted in good faith. Through my connections with some of the leading men in the republic I know only too well how vitally important all matters pertaining to national defence are to you. In a modest way I have even been trying to help here and there. You acted quite correctly, and I shall not hesitate to say so if anybody asks me. But I do suggest you put up a barrier of some sort at the crossroads to prevent incidents of this kind.'

'Yes, yes. Colonel Sabri mentioned it also. It will be done right away. Now it is past twelve o'clock and before you go on you must give us the pleasure of your company at lunch.' He opened the door and stood aside. 'If you will be good enough to come with me. Our officers' club here at the base is small and very modest, but we will do our best to make you welcome.'

The buzzer on his desk sounded again. 'One moment please,' he said, walking across the room to take the call. 'What is it? I am going to lunch now and don't wish to be disturbed. What? ... Yes Sir, yes Sir ...' There was another lengthy session of 'Yes Sirs' and 'Khader Effendim' until finally he held out the instrument to me: 'General Osman on the line for you, Mr Lotz.'

'Hello – Rusty, you old devil what are you up to? Sabri just called me, told me all about your spying out our missile bases. Will you pay a bottle of champagne voluntarily as ransom or do I let you rot in prison?' His laughter boomed at me over the wire and I moved the instrument a little away from my ear.

'If it's local champagne – OK,' I responded.

'Oh no, my friend, I won't let you be a Jew! The French stuff or nothing! Seriously, Rusty, how are they treating you? Any trouble?'

'None at all. Everybody is very nice and understanding. The Commandant has kindly invited us to lunch. After that we are coming straight back to Cairo.'

'Good. Just tell me if there's anything else you want. By the way, Abdo and I and some of the other boys are throwing a stag party next Thursday. Do you think you will be able to get away for an evening? It will be most interesting.'

'I think that might be arranged.'

'Don't miss it. I'm telling you it will be very, very interesting.'

'Like the one we had in Garden City last year?'

'Better. Much better. All the trimmings. OK, I just wanted to know if you are all right. See you Thursday or perhaps before then.'

The Commandant glanced at me sideways as we were walking down the corridor. 'General Osman is very fond of you. It is indeed a pleasure to have you here as our guest, Colonel Lotz.'

'Did you call me Colonel? I was a Captain in the army, and that ages ago.'

'Of course, Sir, if you say so I will not pry into your affairs. Yours is a secret to be proud of. The SS, they tell me, was the crême de la crême of the German Reich. I have read a great deal about it. We too will have a great Arab Reich one day. Installations like our missile base here will help to destroy Israel soon. Now you understand why we guard it so carefully. The Israelis have an excellent intelligence service. They must not learn anything about this until we strike the final blow. Now let me show you around.'

Lotz (on the right) commands the guard of honour during General Sir Brian Robertson's visit to Israel in 1950. General Ezer Weizman is on the extreme left, General Haim Laskow behind.

Lotz leaves Venice for Egypt on the *Ausonia*, 1961.

General of Police, Youssef Ghorab

Left to right: Waltraud, Ahmal, Hamza Pasha (minister of agriculture under Farouk), Madame Wigdane El-Barbary ('Danny') and Dr Mahmoud Ragham Fahmy.

General Abdul Salam ('Abdo').

Wolfgang and Waltraud Lotz at
Cairo's Sahara City Night Club, 1961.

Brenner (right) with one of his assistants.

Dr Pilz.

Salah Nasr, Chief of Egyptian Intelligence.

At a Cavalry Club fancy dress party in 1961, the Lotz's win first prize as Anthony and Cleopatra.

The Lotz's with general at the Cairo Cavalry Club.

The Lotz's villa at Giza, Cairo.

Waltraud and Wolfgang ride Isis and Doctor beneath the palm trees of their horse farm - strategically situated near kilometre 33 and the experimental base.

Lotz races General Ghorab over an obstacle.

(l. to r.) Marcelle Ninio, Philip Nathonson, Lotz, Robert Dassa.

Victor Levy.

Lotz during the Ceremony.

Nadia and Franz Kiesow in court
with the Lotz's.

The second day of the trial: Hasan El-Badawi, President of the court, cross-examines
Lotz about his transmitter. The president has before him the 1,800-page protocol
compiled during Lotz's interrogation.

Lotz demonstrates his transmitter to the court. His
'bathroom scales' are on the table.

The Wedding of the Spies, Tel-Aviv 1971: Prime Minister Golda Meir talks to
Marcelle Ninio, the bride she has just given away, and Marcelle's husband Eli.
Moshe Dayan is on the right.

An official picture of Lotz, released at the time of his arrest and captioned: 'Israel's agent Wolfgang Lotz waiting on a secret appointment with Israeli Intelligence agents abroad.' According to Lotz, it was in fact taken in Venice by Waltraud during their honeymoon.

8

Over and Out

I was restless that night, waking up frequently and looking at my watch. Twice during the night I made sure the alarm clock was set properly, but for once I did not need it. Ten minutes before transmission time I was all set, flexing my fingers in preparation, the message ready before me: MISSILE BASE CONFIRMED BY OWN OBSERVATION STOP EXACT LOCATION. . . .

The reply from the chief came the next morning: RE-CEIVED YOUR FOUR-O-ONE STOP CONGRATULATIONS ON WONDERFUL JOB AND THANKS.

A few days later I went to the bachelor party. I had written down the address on a slip of paper, but not being quite sure I had the right place I sounded my horn. Abdo's head and shoulders appeared over the balcony on the upper floor.

'Oh, it's you, Rusty. Come on in, we're just getting comfortable. Ali, show the bey in.' The boab came running to open the gate for me. I followed him up the brightly lit garden path and was bowed into the entrance hall, where Abdo greeted me with a hearty handshake.

'I'm glad you could come,' he said, putting his arm around my shoulders and leading me into a large salon furnished

in Oriental style and with thick carpets covering every inch
of the floor and low divans all along the walls. A truly magnificent crystal chandelier hung from the ceiling with only
two bulbs turned on, leaving the room in semi-darkness.
Near the door stood a television set. At the other side of
the room a large marble-topped table had been set up as a
bar, with bottles, glasses and two silver buckets filled with
ice cubes. About half a dozen men had already arrived and
were standing in a group near the bar, glasses in hand and
in animated conversation.

'Make yourself at home,' said my host. 'I think you know
everyone here.'

Indeed I did. I saw Fouad talking intensively to Admiral
Fawzi and Mohsen Sabri. Another naval officer, a four-
striper whose name I had forgotten though he had been introduced to me once, and Abdul Karim Halawany, like our
host a Colonel in the Armoured Corps, were pouring the
ingredients of a cocktail into a large silver shaker. Yes – it
looked a promising evening of debauchery – debauchery that
might give me some interesting items of information.

Fouad saw me first and threw back his head, breaking into
laughter. 'Well, hello! – Here comes the spy!' They all
turned their heads in my direction. I had expected some
remark of this kind from Fouad and steeled myself for the
predictable banter.

'If it's the ransom you're looking for,' I said to Fouad,
'I have a case of champagne in the car outside. Have one of
the servants fetch it. Actually I owe you only one bottle
but I thought I might as well bring something a little more
substantial for this thirsty crowd of hard-drinking Mos-
lems.'

Fouad embraced me. 'Three cheers for the spy!' he
shouted. 'Listen, fellows, this is a scream. Our illustrious
friend here went for a picnic to one of the missile bases near
the Canal and I had to bail him out when they arrested him.'

In his clowning manner he gave the others a short account

of the whole affair, evoking a great deal of laughter at my expense. Abdo came in from the next room.

'Where have you been?' I asked him, 'everybody is poking fun at me and I need the moral support of a true friend.'

He smiled. 'The unforgivable part of it is that no one seems to have offered you a drink yet. Whisky?'

Later Abdo ushered us into the dining-room where we took our places around a heavy oak table which could easily seat twenty people or more. In keeping with Egyptian custom the whole meal was already set out. This way of serving food was disagreeable to most Europeans who liked their meals hot, but – as I had often noticed in the past – the Egyptians were quite indifferent to the temperature of their food. It had to be plentiful, well spiced and dripping with oil. Our host had really done us proud tonight. Hardly an inch of the huge table could be seen for the many dishes that covered it. There was a whole roast lamb, a baked turkey, chickens, any number of stuffed pigeons, veal cutlets and escalopes, with side dishes of roast potatoes, rice with almonds and raisins, boiled peas and carrots, tehina, and a large variety of salads. No wine was served, but several bottles of whisky stood on the table and the champagne I had brought was being cooled in ice buckets.

'A meal fit for a king,' I remarked as we seated ourselves.

'A meal fit for good republicans,' Osman corrected me, drawing an ironic smile from Abdo. Our eyes met and he winked at me. With the ever-increasing food shortage in Egypt and prices soaring one had to make a career of being a good republican in order to be able to serve one's guests a meal of such dimensions. It couldn't possibly be done on the pay of a Colonel, somewhat less than a hundred pounds a month.

Our host either came from a rich family and had enough influence to retain his wealth at a time when the property of all so-called 'feudalists' was being sequestrated, or else he had other sources of income. I knew that a lot of officers were

getting rich smuggling hashish from the Gaza strip into
Egypt, but Osman was stationed here in Cairo, at Armoured
Corps Headquarters. Bribery was a possibility, but bribery
was more the line of police and government officials. Who
would want to bribe a Colonel in the Armoured Corps?
Interesting thought, that! I decided to make a mental note
of it for future reference. If Osman was as corrupt as I
hoped, his love of money might be put to good use. I decided
to cultivate his friendship a little more in future.

'You are not eating, fellows. Is this the best you can do?'
Osman was saying. Although we had all eaten heartily and
had had plenty to drink, we had only made a medium-
sized dent in the mountain of food before us. There was
enough left over to feed a whole family for a week.

'It was a wonderful dinner, Osman,' said Fouad, stroking
his stomach with a sigh, 'but I couldn't have another bite.
I'm ready to burst now.' Admiral Fawzi belched delicately,
holding a hand to his mouth, then downed half a water
glass of whisky.

'I haven't eaten like this in years,' he said, 'but enough is
enough. I'll go on a diet tomorrow.'

'You may find gastritis a good excuse to extend your stay
in Cairo for another week or two,' I told him. 'It was
delicious, but I have also eaten too much, couldn't resist it.'

'And now we shall listen to Omm Kolsoum for a while,'
Osman announced, pressing a button on the television set.
My heart sank. This was too much! I dropped heavily on
to a sofa next to Abdo and resigned myself to my fate. Omm
Kolsoum, the Arabian nightingale as she was called, was –
and had been for many years – the most famous and cele-
brated singer of love songs throughout the Arab world. On
the first Thursday of each month she went on the air from
ten o'clock until early morning and wherever there was a
television set men would sit for endless hours listening to her
as though hypnotized, swaying from side to side with their
eyes half-closed, singing and moaning with pleasure.

I took a packet of Players out of my pocket and prepared to light one when Osman stopped me. 'Hold it,' he said, 'I have something far better to offer my guests.' He produced a packet of cigarette papers, some tobacco and a round wooden box which he opened and held under my nose. I sniffed at the brownish yeast-like substance: hashish. There was enough there to get us all twenty-five years in prison.

Penalties for hashish smoking were exceedingly stiff in the United Arab Republic. Nasser was trying hard to inject some efficiency into his sluggish people and to improve their standard of living by pulling them out of their perpetual hashish stupor; but it was no use. Millions of Egyptians would let their families starve, spending their last piastre on the drug and risking long terms of imprisonment, rather than do without their daily smoke.

'Roll yourself a cigarette, Rusty,' my host was saying, 'it will make you feel better. It's good for the digestion too.'

'I'm not very used to it,' I answered, 'but I'll have a small one. It should go well with Omm Kolsoum.'

I took a leaf of the thin rice paper, put some tobacco and a pinch of hashish on it, and rolled it into a cigarette. The box was passed round and all the others helped themselves liberally.

Abdo sitting next to me inhaled deeply. 'Great stuff,' he remarked, 'Osman has tons of it.'

'Where does he get it?' I asked. 'Isn't he afraid of being found out?'

He smiled knowingly: 'Osman served for years in Sinai and has the connections. Now he supplies the Marshal regularly, so what can happen to him? How do you think he got this cushy job at HQ and jumped from Major to Colonel in a year! Look at the way he lives. Like a prince.' He got up and poured us both another stiff drink. 'This will be more to your taste than hashish I think.'

*   *   *

Half an hour later Abdo and I entered the Champagne Club, situated in the basement of the Hotel Cosmopolitan. We had been delegated to pick up some tarts – to take back to the so-called bachelor party. The place had retained its high-sounding name from the days of the monarchy when it had been the most extravagant nightclub in Cairo. Dozens of glamorous mannequins from Paris and Rome used to populate the bar and exhibit their charms on the dance floor. Only the richest of pashas, beys and foreign visitors could afford to be members. All this had changed drastically under the Nasser régime. The once famous Champagne Club had become a third-rate dive visited mainly by tourists. A ragged looking five-piece band was playing off-key jazz and a number of girls in cheap evening gowns were available as dancing partners. A floor show of sorts was put on twice during the night to give the girls the status of 'artistes'. Three of them were listlessly leaning on the bar when we came in, four others sat together at a nearby table smoking. The place was almost empty. Abdo drew me to the bar. 'We'll have a drink first,' he said, 'this is thirsty work.' He signalled to the barman who stopped cleaning his nails and came over.

'Ahmad, I want two double whiskies. No, no, not this stuff. Bring a new bottle of Johnny Walker and let me see it before you open it, you thief.' He inspected the sealed bottle carefully and finally gave his approval.

One of the girls at the bar, a tall brunette and pretty in spite of her tired look and excessive make-up, moved over to Abdo's side, putting her arm around his waist.

Abdo looked the girls over. 'I suggest we take the lot from here and don't bother about the tarts from the Continental. Saves time. What do you think, Rusty?'

'Suits me. But do you think there'll be enough to go round? Personally I'm not keen on any of this.'

'Better off at home, eh? Well, these will have to do. Some

of the boys will be too drunk anyway, and if we're short
we can always double park.'

He waved his arm at the other girls who came over eagerly.
As we all moved towards the exit there was a commotion at
the door. Two waiters were trying to restrain a large bulky
man who shook them off with some effort, shouting at the
top of his voice:

'Let me go, let me go, you bastards! Where is she? Where
is that rotten bitch?'

Abdo and I both recognized him. He was a minor official
at the American Embassy whom we'd often seen at the club.

'What's the matter, Bill?' I asked, 'don't get excited.'

'What's the matter?! Don't get excited? Listen you, I
spent seven pounds on this lousy bitch and she promised to
meet me outside. Where is she? Does she think she can put
one over on me? I'll show her a thing or two! Where is
she?'

'Pipe down,' Bill,' I tried to calm him, 'you're drunk.
Better go and sleep it off.'

'Drunk? Sure I'm drunk!' He pulled out a jacknife and
snapped it open.

'Now listen, you bastards,' he shouted, 'I spent seven
pounds on this whore and if she doesn't come and give me
my money's worth I'm going to carve myself seven pounds
of whore's ass, see?'

He made a move towards one of the girls, waving the
open blade at her menacingly. She screamed and ran out.
Quickly I took hold of his arm, wrested the knife away
from him, and gave his arm an additional twist so that he
drunkenly collapsed on the floor. He looked up at me in
dazed surprise.

By the time we got back to Osman's, the belly dancer with
her three-piece orchestra of violin, drums and a kind of
guitar had arrived and was already in full swing – in the
literal sense of the word. She was performing in the centre

H

of the large salon accompanied by hand-clapping and
encouraging calls from the men. She was wearing the usual
embroidered brassière and panties with a long transparent
train split at the sides. The so-called 'Nasser's curtain', an
austere covering for the dancer's back and abdomen, which
was prescribed by law for public performances, had been
dispensed with.

Our entrance with the cabaret girls was cheered loudly by
everybody. Introductions were performed merrily by exchanging kisses and the girls were treated to glasses of champagne in quick succession 'to warm up the engines', as Fawzi
put it. One by one Osman's guests retired with their tarts.
Relieved, and nursing a vile headache, I moved towards the
door.

'I'll be on my way,' I said to Fouad.

'But why, Rusty? Aren't you having any of the
girls?'

'Frankly, Fouad, I prefer my sex in private.'

'Suit yourself, old boy. I shall spend the night here. By
the way, there's something I want to ask you before you
go. A small favour. We have some new Germans arriving
next week, electronic experts for a hush-hush project connected with missiles. It will probably take them a little while
to settle down and you know their German ways better
than we do. I'll introduce you to them and I want you to
keep an eye on them for a week or two to see what they're
like, privately. I mean, what they think about our régime,
what they talk about among themselves, and so on. The other
German experts wouldn't tell me things like that – they all
stick together like glue. I have to use a man I can trust. Will
you do me this small favour, Rusty?'

I pretended to chew it over. 'Well, Fouad, to be quite
candid I don't know what to say. I find the idea of spying
on my own countrymen a little distasteful.'

'But it's not spying Rusty,' he answered. 'You'll be protecting your adopted country. You're already half an

Egyptian and your heart is with us. You'd be doing me a
great personal service.'

'Well, of course I realize it's important to you and the
war effort. If you're asking me to do it as an act of friendship, then I can't refuse. But it must remain strictly between
us. That's the condition.'

'But most certainly, Rusty! I give you my word. Nobody shall ever hear about this.'

On my way out I gleefully smacked the firm behind of
a neat brunette. There is a proverb in German: 'It does not
matter if you are not beautiful or clever, but you have to
be lucky.'

*   *   *

At this point I became involved in a farcical but highly
dangerous situation through my association with a couple
called Bolter. The husband, Dr Heinrich Bolter, a German,
was an archaeologist and head of a Yale expedition then in
Egypt. Most of the year he was away working in Upper
Egypt, while his wife and small child remained in Cairo,
living in a villa not far from ours.

The wife, Caroline, claimed to be half Dutch and half
Hungarian and although she spoke fluent German she always denied any links with Germany. Because she was alone
in a foreign country, we often invited her to our parties,
together with other Europeans and Germans. But after a
while we became suspicious of her, largely because she was
always angling for information about the rocket industry.
Time and again she would steer the conversation to rockets,
asking very directly where they were located, how many
and how powerful they were, and so on. I also noticed that
whenever she was slightly drunk she relapsed into Yiddish!

Again, Caroline Bolter tried in a very obvious way to
strike up a friendship with Marlis Knupfer. Although she
lived at the other end of Cairo, Caroline Bolter joined the

Heleopolis Sporting Club, which was about an hour's drive
from her home, so that she would meet Mrs Knupfer there.
She never went to the sporting clubs near her home, which
was equally strange.

Karl Knupfer's office was right next to his house, in Nasser
City. From his bedroom there was a perfect view of the
room in his office where rocket plans were drawn and
where the detailed diagrams were kept. For this reason,
presumably, Knupfer always kept the shutters of his bedroom window closed when he was out and the door locked
– though for some reason the key was left in the lock.

One night, well after midnight, Karl – normally a cautious
man who kept himself to himself – appeared at my home.
He was in a highly nervous state and visibly shaken. He
told me he was convinced Caroline Bolter was an Israeli
spy. I registered surprise but listened intently as he went on
to relate the day's events.

Caroline Bolter had met his wife as usual at the Sporting
Club. Later she'd left the club with her, asking for a lift and
attaching herself in a way that made it impossible for Mrs
Knupfer not to ask her back for a drink – at least not without being blatantly rude. She'd left Caroline Bolter in the
living-room and gone into the kitchen to give some instructions to her cook. When she returned, Caroline was not
there. Puzzled, Mrs Knupfer began to search the flat for
her – eventually discovering her in the bedroom, the door
unlocked, the shutters open. What's more, she was in the
process of taking photographs from the bedroom window.
Caroline blushed, and stammered some excuse about looking
for her child's ball, which she thought was somewhere in
the flat. . . .

Karl Knupfer knew I was well connected and wanted my
advice. He was particularly worried because of some recent
sabotage activities of Israeli Intelligence and thought he
should report the whole matter to the Egyptian security
authorities. Naturally, I now realized that Caroline Bolter

might indeed be working for Israeli Intelligence, and though it meant sticking my own neck out I decided I must prevent her arrest. I told Knupfer that since he had not even bothered to collect the film from her camera he had no real evidence. He could give only a vague report which could not be substantiated with concrete evidence. Nobly, I offered to take the matter in hand saying that I would ask my contacts in Egyptian security to keep her under surveillance until there was enough rope to hang her. Knupfer, only too glad to pass on the responsibility, readily agreed.

Next morning I transmitted the following message to Israel:

MOST URGENT STOP CHIEF PERSONAL STOP CAROLINE BOLTER CAUGHT RED-HANDED BY KNUPFER PHOTOGRAPHING HIS OFFICE FROM BEDROOM WINDOW STOP KNUPFER AGREED LEAVE MATTERS IN MY HANDS NOT REPORT AUTHORITIES STOP OBVIOUSLY SHE WORKS FOR SOME ORGANIZATION STOP IF FOR OURS SUGGEST WITHDRAWAL IMMEDIATELY STOP

The very next afternoon Caroline received a cable from her 'aunt' in Germany, saying that she was critically ill and that she should return home. She left with her child the same night. The following morning I received this message:

THANK YOU YOUR 401 STOP ALL TAKEN CARE OF STOP

*   *   *

A few days after the Caroline Bolter incident, Fouad called on me. He wanted to know whether I'd got anywhere with the German electronic experts he'd asked me to watch. He also questioned me about Knupfer, which, in view of recent events, put me on my guard.

'I haven't forgotten your request, habibi,' I told him. 'As it happens I've seen quite a bit of the new aircraft people in the past few weeks, and of Knupfer too, of course. What do you want to know about Karl? His technical qualifications . . .'

'. . . are first class, we made sure of that, but we don't know anything else about him, nothing to point to his character, that is.'

'He's a rather shy and withdrawn man. He's strict with his subordinates and has hardly any social contact with them. One thing, he never speaks about his work to outsiders.'

This was perfectly true, but I omitted to say that his wife was the one who gave me precise up-to-date information on everything her husband did – as she had done, for instance, about Traum and Eberhard. Once she started to talk, nothing could stop her.

'That's a good point,' Fouad was saying. 'What does he think about the régime?'

'To be quite frank, Fouad, he doesn't care for it. All I ever hear from him is criticism. Give him time, he'll change.'

This was a deliberate lie. Knupfer may have been an excellent engineer, but he showed no interest whatsoever in politics. He had a well-paid position, lived in luxury and was able to save money into the bargain. Nothing else mattered to him and he had certainly no complaints to make about the United Arab Republic that paid him so handsomely. But I had good reasons for telling Fouad a tale that would arouse his suspicions. Knowing the Egyptians, I could be certain that from now on Knupfer would be hampered in his work. He would be carefully observed, everything he did or said would be suspect and questioned. I knew that the Egyptians, who were wily but never subtle, would soon succeed in irritating him to such an extent that he would be unable to work properly. I had seen other important projects go down the drain through the mutual distrust of foreign experts and their Egyptian employers.

*   *   *

The following two weeks were hectic and tiring. Apart from routine operations – observing and reporting developments in the military sphere – I had on my hands a group of German riders and horsebreeders who had come to Egypt on what was termed a 'hippological' study trip.

Some months earlier I had, at the request of the German Horsebreeders' Association, suggested this study trip to the Egyptian authorities, who were delighted by the idea and asked me to organize the whole tour and act as liaison officer between them and the visiting group. The German consulate was none too helpful, but fortunately the Egyptians, who loved showing off their country to foreigners, were most accommodating. A rather impressive programme was arranged which included visits to the government stud farm, visits to private racing stables and farms where pure Arab horses were bred, displays of horsemanship by mounted units of the police with subsequent inspection of the police academy and a performance of trained police dogs, a jumping competition of cavalry teams, a reception at the racing club – and a round of cocktail parties, teas and interminable speeches. Acting as manager, guide, interpreter, lecturer, and even shopping adviser to the group kept me on my toes from early morning until late at night and interfered with my work; but afterwards the Egyptian authorities could not do enough to express their gratitude for the part I had played in cementing the traditional German-Egyptian friendship. As a result my cover was more firmly established than ever.

The hippological study group – the 'hippos' Waltraud called them – had hardly left when her parents arrived from Germany to celebrate her birthday with us. I got on well with them and always did my best to make them welcome in our home; but at the same time special precautions had to be taken.

On top of all this, the pressure of work was mounting. The United Arab Republic was going through a severe economical and political crisis and plots to assassinate the

President and overthrow the régime were whispered everywhere. Through my contacts in the army, the police and
certain government circles I had acquired extensive and
top secret information not only on the true state of affairs,
which was even worse than the man in the street suspected,
but also on the measures the government was proposing to
take. The implications were far-reaching and I considered it
imperative that my superiors be fully informed with as little
delay as possible. This presented certain problems. The
situation called for reports that would be far too lengthy
and detailed for wireless transmission. I decided after some
deliberation to report in person and began to make preparations for a trip to Europe in early March – about two or
three weeks hence. It was essential to avoid making a hasty
departure which would cause comment and necessitate
elaborate explanation.

Waltraud's birthday party was spread over three days to
accommodate the many guests who wanted to come, but
the first, on February 18, was a small party restricted to the
family and close friends. Proudly Waltraud displayed the
ring I had given her for her birthday, a four-and-a-half-
carat diamond set in platinum, which was duly admired by
everyone. Who was to foresee that it would remain hers for
less than a week!

The other two nights of festivities were, from the professional angle, most rewarding. Among others we had invited a large number of German and Austrian experts, mostly
aircraft builders. By now it was becoming clear that the
local production of military aircraft, on which Nasser had
set such high hopes, had proved a complete flop. Work on
the HA-300 fighter-bomber, which should have been in serial
production long ago, had not even got beyond the experimental stage. Six years and some five hundred millions had
been wasted. The Egyptians accused the foreign experts
of falling down on the job, and they in turn blamed the
Egyptians and each other. Whenever the German air-

craft builders met, this was their main topic of conversation, the subject of much bitter argument which degenerated into out and out rows: the occasion of Waltraud's birthday party was no exception.

It didn't take long. After an opulent buffet dinner and some large drinks they immediately weighed into their favourite subject. Stengel, who was in charge of engine construction, his face growing redder, his voice thicker and his movements unsteadier with every glass, was trying to prove that all was, in fact, as it should be – at least as far as *his* department was concerned.

'So it takes a little longer than we thought,' he shouted, knocking over a bottle with a sweeping movement of his arm. 'That is perfectly natural. We are not an assembly plant putting together a few nuts and screws. We are creating an entirely new type of aircraft that will revolutionize air warfare in the Middle East. You can't do that overnight. We are making satisfactory progress. More than satisfactory!'

Vogelsang laughed derisively. 'Most satisfactory, eh! Then why does your bloody engine break down every time you put it on the test bench for a trial run? Not once or twice, mind you, but every single time. Explain that!'

I leant up against the bar, casually. This was going to be fun.

'You are a fool!' Stengel shouted. 'Since when have you become an engineer? Why don't you stick to your payrolls and rubber stamps! You talk like some of those Egyptian imbeciles I have to work with. The purpose of the test bench is to detect constructional faults and correct them. If you had a grain of technical knowledge you'd know that a prototype engine has to be tested dozens, even hundreds of times and adjustments made after each test.'

Vogelsang tightened his lips. 'Calling me names won't get your plane into the air any faster, Stengel. I may not be a technician, but I do know that yours is the department that's years behind schedule. At the Messerschmitt plant the body is ready down to the last screw. All it needs is an engine to make it fly; but perhaps you consider that an unimportant detail?'

'The Messerschmitt people ready? You must be drunk. They're no more ready than we are. And I'll tell you why.'

For a good twenty minutes he gave a precise outline of production procedure and a summary of technical data which was supplemented by some of the other engineers. Excusing myself, I went to the toilet to jot down the main points. Later I would memorize the information at leisure and burn my notes.

Returning from my solitary labour I rejoined the group at the bar. Stengel and Vogelsang were still at daggers drawn, with the others taking sides. Stengel's wife, a skinny blonde who hardly ever opened her mouth in her husband's presence, came up behind me and touched my arm.

'Do me a favour, Mr Lotz,' she whispered, 'don't give Erich so much to drink. You know how difficult he becomes when he has had too much.'

She had spoken quietly but Stengel, despite his intoxicated state, had overheard her remark. 'Mind your own damn business!' he shouted at her. 'Get back to the other hens and stop pestering Mr Lotz. Difficult am I? I'll show you how difficult I can be when we get home!'

'None of us have any doubts that you will,' remarked Vogelsang pointedly. Mrs Stengel blushed scarlet and left the room hurriedly.

'What do you mean by that?' asked Stengel, hitting the bar with his clenched fist. 'I want an answer, Vogelsang!'

'You do?' Vogelsang's voice held a note of deep contempt. 'Anybody here could answer. We all know how you beat your wife, Mr Chief Engineer! How you have fights with your son when he tries to stop you knocking his mother about – so don't give us this injured innocence act.'

'You dirty Viennese pimp, I'll teach you manners!' Sten-

gel jumped off his bar stool and made for Vogelsang. I
stepped between them.

'Gentlemen, gentlemen! Have the courtesy not to brawl
in my house.'

'That's right,' said Brenner, getting up and moving his
bulk in front of Stengel. 'Settle your differences in private,
not here. Sit down, Stengel, and behave. You too, Vogelsang. I absolutely forbid another word on this subject!'

'We will change the subject,' answered Vogelsang stiltedly,
'out of respect for our host and hostess and not because you
take it upon yourself to "forbid it", Mr Brenner. Unless I
am greatly mistaken you will not be in a position either to
forbid or permit anything around here much longer.'

'Now, what is that supposed to mean?' asked Brenner
aggressively.

'Come, come Brenner, no offence intended, but try to be
objective. How many of us do you think will remain in
Egypt for any length of time? The exodus is already in
full swing.'

'Unfortunately that's true,' put in Hoffman, another department head. 'In my section we're already short of two
engineers and a technician. Another three told me only this
morning that I can expect their resignations early in the
summer. If I don't get replacements I'll have to close shop.'

'Yes, summer will be the critical period,' remarked Hertz,
a former Luftwaffe pilot, who also headed one of the
engineering sections. 'I suspect that many of the boys won't
return from their holidays.'

'But why?' shouted Brenner. 'Why are they doing this
to me? What's wrong with the job? Aren't these young
bucks well enough off? Their salary is treble what it would
be in Germany and six times what they'd get in Austria.
The work is interesting and hardly strenuous, they have
luxury apartments, servants, expensive cars, customs and currency privileges – I just don't understand them.'

Hertz laughed. 'For old-timers like us these are excellent

reasons for staying here as long as we can. But some of these youngsters have different ideas. They've come to realize that there's no future here for them, they're fed up with the squalor and lack of facilities and lies and thievery and corruption. Quite a few of them are also afraid.'

'Afraid? Of what?'

'Of being blown to bits by the Israelis, of course.'

Slowly, I lit a cigarette, drawing in deeply, and half closing my eyes.

'That's a lot of rubbish,' Brenner was saying.

'I don't think it is. Anyone but a blind man can see the writing on the wall.'

'Yes,' said Hoffman, 'you put it a little dramatically, but on the whole you are right, Vogelsang. All the same I'm for holding out as long as we can.'

'Quite right,' said Brenner, sticking out his chest, 'we must stand by our Egyptian friends.' He looked up in astonishment, baffled by the general outburst of laughter his words had provoked.

'To hell with that,' retorted Hoffman. 'They have made a mess of things and we owe them nothing. As for the future? Well, there are plenty of other countries that need aircraft experts.'

'You might find employment in Israel,' jibed Hertz amidst more laughter.

'Why not? Do you think I wouldn't go there if the pay was right? I'm an engineer, not a politician. Give me a good contract and I'll work anywhere.'

Brenner pushed his empty glass away and stood up. 'I've had enough of this,' he announced. 'It's late and I'm going home.'

'I take it you don't share Mr Hoffman's views,' Vogelsang threw at him, grinning.

'I consider his last remarks in exceedingly poor taste. . . . A word of advice, Hoffman: this kind of wild talk might get you into trouble. I suggest you button up your lips in

future, drunk or sober.' He turned to me. 'Goodnight, horseman. It's been a most enjoyable party. Please excuse my
colleagues' behaviour – they don't mean any harm. We are
all under a good deal of strain these days. Now where's
your wife?'

An hour later the last of the guests staggered from our
home.

'That's another day's work done,' remarked Waltraud.
'I was afraid they'd stay for breakfast.'

'Yes it was a rough evening – but it's clear that the much-
publicized aircraft industry will never be a threat to anyone.
I have a feeling that the same holds true for their rockets.
I'll have to see Knupfer and Schwamm about that. There'll
be a lot to tell when I meet the boss next month.'

I climbed into bed and went straight to sleep. Oddly I
dreamed of a small animal in a gin trap.

* * *

A few days later, the Knupfers and Waltraud's parents
joined us on a trip to Mersa Matrouh. Youssef Ghorab
had been begging us for some while now to pay him another
visit, and it seemed a good opportunity to cement our growing friendship with the Knupfers and incidentally show our
visitors a little of the country. We went to Alexandria by
the Delta road, Waltraud's parents in our car and the Knupfers following in theirs. They had seen very little of the
country as yet and were glad to have me as a guide. We
spent the afternoon sight-seeing and taking photographs of
each other, and in the evening I took them to the Santa
Lucia Bar where I succeeded in making Knupfer drink almost half a bottle of whisky. This proved to be too much.
Instead of becoming talkative, as I'd hoped, he turned green
in the face and was promptly sick.

'Better luck next time,' I said to Waltraud. 'I'll have to
pace it more carefully in future.'

Arriving at Mersa Matrouh after an hour-long drive through the desert, our little convoy drew up in front of the Governor's mansion. A squad of policemen armed with rifles stood in formation near the entrance gate. At our approach a bugle sounded, the police squad presented arms and General Youssef Ghorab came down the steps to welcome his guests. After being duly kissed and embraced by Youssef, I introduced Waltraud's parents and Mr and Mrs Knupfer, who were visibly impressed. At luncheon, an elaborate eight course meal, Youssef expressed regret at our short stay.

'What? Only one day?' he exclaimed. 'Rusty, I have all sorts of things laid on for you. Dinner-parties, fishing, visits to the Bedouin tribes, a gymkhana with horses and riding camels, a million things. You can't do all that in a day! You must stay a week, two weeks. My daughter, Hannah, wants to thank you personally for the great joy you have given her.'

Noticing Marlis Knupfer's astonished glance, he hastened to explain: 'You see, Madame, I have three daughters, Inis, Nagwa, and Hannah. It was God's will that I should have only daughters, but they are the best daughters a man could wish for, intelligent, healthy and beautiful. Unfortunately, my youngest, Hannah, who is nineteen now, has inherited her father's nose, large and hooked like an eagle's beak. For a man a nose like this is no handicap, on the contrary, they say it shows character. For a young girl, though, it amounts to a tragedy. But my daughter was very fortunate that her father has a friend like Mr Lotz, a true, unselfish, generous friend. He could not bear to see her unhappy, going through life with a deformity like that, and he moved heaven and earth until he found a plastic surgeon, a German professor, who operated on Hannah. Mr Lotz's birthday gift to my daughter was the thing she had most wanted all her life, a nose of classical beauty. You will meet Hannah tomorrow. Thank you again, Rusty, and please don't think about leaving so soon.'

I explained that my father-in-law had urgent business in Germany and it was finally agreed to extend our visit by one more day.

There followed two days of sightseeing during which we admired new agricultural development projects, met notables and overate. My parents-in-law were particularly amused by what Waltraud termed 'the Lotz Museum'. This was an enormous glass show-case which Youssef had installed in the reception hall of the Governor's mansion. There he kept on display everything I had given him during my stay in Egypt – tape recorders of various sizes, cameras, electric mixers, electric tooth brushes, electric shavers, binoculars, radios, and a great many other items. These were so rare and expensive in Egypt that Youssef had never dreamed of putting them to their intended uses. Instead he displayed them to his many Egyptian guests as proudly as others would a rare painting.

In the early afternoon of February 22, we left for Cairo, rather exhausted. It was a tiring uneventful drive and when we reached the capital we stopped on Pyramid road to say goodbye to the Knupfers. They thanked us effusively for what they called a unique experience, saying they hoped to see much much more of us. We re-entered the car in the best of spirits, smiling and waving as we turned the corner into our street.

'The home stretch at last,' I remarked, letting the car roll to a stop in front of the gate. 'I suggest we make this an early night. I think we could all do with a solid ten hours sleep.'

Suddenly I saw four cars, full of men, parked on the opposite side of the street. The men were just about to get out.

'What's going on?' I said jokingly, as we got out of the car. 'The neighbours must be having a party.'

The words were hardly out of my mouth when I received a stunning blow on the head that felled me to my knees. I heard Waltraud cry out. About six men jumped on me, knocking me to the ground. My head was swimming. Before I fully realized what was happening, handcuffs closed on my wrists and I was pulled roughly to my feet.

9
The Truth, Mr Lotz

'Take them inside. Quickly, this is attracting too much attention. Keep them separated.' The orders were barked out by a short, very fat man with eyeglasses. The garden gate and the front door were unlocked and I was half-carried, half-dragged into the house. In our living-room I was made to sit in an armchair with a man holding me firmly on each side. My head was clearing now and I looked round for Waltraud and her parents.

'Where is my wife?' I asked.

The room was full of people and I couldn't see her anywhere. A smallish man with a black moustache, who was wearing sunglasses although it was already dark outside, looked down at me with a grim expression.

'She is not here,' he said harshly. 'You will not see her for a long time, perhaps never again. It will be better for you to tell us everything. We know you are a spy. Who are the other members of your ring? Give us the names of your accomplices.'

'Who are you?' I shouted at him. 'What's all this about? How dare you manhandle me in my own house!'

He slapped my face twice with the back of his hand.

'Don't speak to me like that. You know exactly why we are here.'

The fat one came over, pushing the others aside. 'Let me handle this, Hassan Bey. You can have him later.' Then he addressed me in English: 'I am Samir Nagy, Prosecutor-General for State Security. You are under arrest.'

'Under arrest? What for?'

'You don't know? I think you have a pretty good idea why we've arrested you, Mr Lotz.'

'Don't be ridiculous! What on earth would anyone want to arrest me for? Give me the telephone and we'll have this idiotic mistake cleared up in no time at all.'

'You think so? Whom do you wish to call, Mr Lotz?'

'First of all the German Ambassador. I shall submit a strong complaint about the manner in which German citizens are treated by these thugs of yours.'

'I advise you to be more careful in your choice of words, Mr Lotz. You may regret it.'

'We'll see later who does the regretting, Mr Nagy. Give me that phone.'

'Who are the other people you want to call? Friends of yours?'

'Yes, very good friends. One is the Governor of the Western District. He will vouch for me.'

'General Ghorab is already on his way to Cairo. Unfortunately he is in no position to vouch for anyone.'

'What do you mean?'

'He has been arrested as an accomplice. We shall soon find out exactly how he was connected with you. Did he work for you?'

'This is too stupid for words! You barge in here with fantastic allegations about my being a spy, you frighten my wife and relatives, you slander my friends – on what basis? What proof have you for your preposterous accusations? If you want to know exactly who I am, lift the phone yourself. Call General Fouad Osman, call General Abdel

Salaam Suleiman, call Colonel Mohsen Sabri, call. . . .'

He interrupted me with a smile and shake of his head.
'It's no good, Mr Lotz. Your bluff won't work this time.
We know all about the gentlemen you mention and your
other friends too. Their interrogation will reveal just how
far they are implicated, whether they are active accomplices
or only the stupid and careless victims of your clever schemes.
Yes, you are clever Mr Lotz, I grant you that, but we have
one of the best intelligence services in the world. How long
did you imagine you could go on fooling us?'

'Listen. . . .'

He held up his hand. 'I will listen to what you have to
say for many days and nights, I promise you, whether you
like it or not. Just now we have other things to do.' He
motioned to the men. 'Search everything!'

At least ten of them spread out through the ground floor
to conduct a search. As far as I could see they were not
making a very thorough job of it. My hopes rose, for unless
they discovered the wireless transmitter in the bathroom scales they would not have a shred of evidence against
me. On the other hand they seemed too sure of
themselves for comfort. They were bound to be on to something.

I was racking my brains, trying to think of what might
have gone wrong – a leakage somewhere, something incriminating they could have come across. There was nothing
I could put my finger on, certainly nothing that would have
justified this full-dress invasion of my home and the cock-
sure behaviour of the invaders. All-powerful as the Security
Police might be in Egypt, they would hardly go so far as to
beat up and arrest a wealthy foreigner and his family on
mere suspicion. There had to be something more substantial
than that. But what? I watched them opening drawers and
cupboards, turning over chairs and taking down pictures
from the walls. It was done rather perfunctorily and after
a short while the searchers reported that nothing suspicious

had been found. Appearing in no way disappointed, Samir
Nagy acknowledged the information.

He led the way up the stairs to our bedroom and I
followed with my two guards hanging on to my arms. The
others came up behind. Nagy seated himself on a chair in
front of my small writing desk.

'A large, beautiful bedroom,' he remarked. 'What have
you got in those cupboards?' He pointed to a row of four
huge mahogany cupboards with yale locks. It was the accepted thing in Egypt to lock everything of value away
whenever one left the house, because of the servants whose
honesty could not always be relied upon.

'They contain clothes and household articles,' I replied.

'I see. Have you got the key to this cupboard here?' He
indicated the second from the right, the one where I kept
some electrical appliances as well as my bathroom scales.

'The keys are in my pocket,' I answered. 'If you remove
these handcuffs I'll give them to you.'

'Thank you, but we can manage by ourselves – Mahfous,
search him and empty his pockets.' The man he had addressed went through my pockets, removing my wallet, keys,
identity papers, cigarette case, lighter and some change, plac-
ing everything on the desk in front of Nagy, who inspected
every item.

'You carry a lot of money, Mr Lotz. Why?'

'It is my money, I didn't steal it.'

'Heaven forbid! A gentleman like you has no need to
steal. The Israeli Intelligence are paying you very well.'

'You must be out of your mind!'

'You think so? All right, let's open this cupboard and see
what we find.' He handed the keys to Mahfous who unlocked the cupboard door and opened it.

'Ah, you have a nice collection of electrical household
appliances,' said Nagy. 'Very useful. And what is this? Bathroom scales! Do you weigh yourself on these scales every
morning, Mr Lotz?'

'Every morning! Do you want to weigh yourself too? Be my guest.'

'No thank you, Mr Lotz. It would only make me sad to see how much I weigh. Also,' he added with heavy sarcasm, 'I would not wish to break the delicate mechanism, one can't be too careful with this kind of equipment.'

'Open this weighing machine,' Nagy said to Mahfous who lifted the lid with a triumphant look, displaying the hidden wireless set. Everything was clear to me now. The lid was normally fastened down by a set of springs and levers and could be opened only with a special key. It had been forced open and loosely replaced in its former position. Samir Nagy stared at me fixedly for some moments, neither of us saying anything. To try and bluff and bluster my way out of this would only have been so much waste of breath. From now on it would be wisest to say as little as possible until I knew how much they had found out, and then play it down as far as I could. Things might not be quite as bad as they seemed. I had to confess something that sounded true, but that would come later. For the moment I needed time to think.

Nagy shrugged his shoulders in an almost apologetic manner and turned away from me, beckoning to a thin bald-headed man who had been standing quietly near the door making notes in a book. 'Take down a protocol, Hamdy.'

When the man had seated himself and indicated that he was ready, Nagy began dictating to him:

'Acting on information received, I, Samir Nagy, Prosecutor-General for State Security, in conjunction with Hassan Aleesh and a unit of State Security Police, have, on February 22, 1965, at 20.30 hours, carried out a search at the residence of one Johann Wolfgang Lotz, a German national, at 11 Sharia Mahmoud Ghaleb in Giza. Concealed inside the bathroom scales was found a set of wireless communication equipment, a cipher key and a typewritten page

containing instructions regarding clandestine wireless transmission. Attached to this protocol are photographs of the
items listed above. The following persons of German
nationality were taken into custody at the above mentioned
time and place: Johann Wolfgang Lotz; his wife, Waltraud
Clara Martha Lotz; her parents, Otto Neumann and Clara
Neumann. When arrested, Wolfgang Lotz denied being engaged in espionage. Confronted with the evidence he made
no further statement. – That's all, Hamdy. Give it to me to
sign and call the photographer.'

When photographs of the room, myself and the wireless
set had been taken from every angle, I was taken down to
one of the waiting cars where I was blindfolded with my
handkerchief. The car took off and drove at great speed for
about half an hour. Once I tried to raise my head, to peep
out from under the blindfold, but all I got for my efforts
was a blow on the back of my neck and a brief order to
sit still. At last the car came to a stop, I heard a gate open
and we drove on for another few yards. I was pushed out
of the car and down four or five steps.

'Keep him there until we are ready,' I heard the voice of
Hassan Aleesh saying. 'Don't speak to him and don't beat
him yet.' Some sort of hood was pulled over my head on
top of the blindfold and I was left standing there for what
must have been well over an hour. Heavy boots were
stamping up and down and someone was talking in whispers.
Then I heard a woman's voice screaming in Arabic:
'W'allahi – by God, I know nothing about it! Nothing, nothing, I swear it by God! Stop it, please stop it! I'll say anything you want but stop it.'

I thought I recognized Nadia Kiesow's voice, but couldn't
be sure. Later I heard my father-in-law saying something
in German a long distance away. Finally somebody came
and, after removing my handcuffs, took me by the sleeve
and told me to follow him. I stumbled down some more
stairs, round two or three corners and through a door.

There I was told to stop and my hood and blindfold were removed. I was in a smallish bare room facing a large desk. Behind it sat Hassan Aleesh flanked by Mahfous and a very tall, athletic-looking man with small, vicious eyes who had been in the car with me and whom I had heard addressed as Abdul Hakim. On my side of the desk there was a kind of piano stool, its one iron leg cemented to the floor. Aleesh bade me sit down on it. It was far from comfortable but better than having to stand. He pressed a button and two powerful projectors came on, their light blurring my eyes and almost blinding me.

'My name is Mahmoud, Mr Lotz,' he said. 'It is not my real name, of course, but it will do for the present. What about you? Is Lotz your real name?'

'Certainly.'

'And you have no other names?'

'Of course not. Why should I have other names?'

'It happens in your profession – or should I say our profession. Look, Lotz, we shall be seeing a great deal of each other in the near future and there is no reason why we should not conduct our conversations in a friendly atmosphere. It will make it easier for both of us, so I strongly advise you to cooperate. Otherwise it will not be very pleasant. But you are far too intelligent not to realize that. As I said, we are members of the same profession. You have been caught. That is hard luck, but it is not the end of the world. We will shake hands like true sportsmen and you will start a new life. We can help you a lot, you know, but you must help us too, as I am sure you will. Instead of hanging you might receive a very light sentence, perhaps two or three years only – it all depends on you. How do you feel now? Would you like some coffee?'

'Yes, thank you.'

He clapped his hands and ordered coffee from the guard who answered his summons. 'Have a cigarette.' He reached into his pocket and put a packet of Belmont on the table. I took one and he lit it for me.

'I would appreciate having my own cigarettes back,' I said.

'Of course. You will have all the cigarettes you want. Now, Mr Lotz, before we begin our discussion I want to show you something. I will convince you it's pointless to tell us any lies. We know all about you.' From a drawer in the desk he extracted two large dossiers which he placed before me. 'Do these look familiar to you? Read them, take your time.'

'Do you mind turning off those lights,' I said, 'I can't see properly.'

He switched them off and I began leafing through the dossiers. There, neatly filed away, were transcripts of my wireless messages dating back several years – that is, as far as I could tell without consulting the code key. Obviously they had been searching hard – and had finally run my transmitter to earth.

'Makes you think doesn't it, Mr Lotz,' said Aleesh. 'We have been monitoring your wireless communications for almost three years.* This dossier here contains the incoming, the other one the outgoing messages. No doubt you can recognize them even in their present form. Now that we have the key our experts are already hard at work decoding them. So you see, we don't actually need your help. The text of the messages will tell us all we want to know about your activities.'

Unfortunately this was true. If they succeeded in decoding even as few as a dozen or so of these messages, which – using my key – was child's play, they would find enough incriminating material to hang me three times over. My only option was to pretend to cooperate up to a point. No useful purpose would be served by keeping silent and deny-

* That was not actually the case. It later became apparent that my messages had been intercepted and my position located through the agents of another power.

ing everything. If they began to use torture, their standard procedure, they were likely to make me reveal more than I had intended. On the other hand, by adopting a cooperative attitude and telling them things they already knew or could easily find out for themselves, I might be able to lead them a little astray and perhaps fling a spanner into the works somewhere along the line. I had my acting abilities – and if I wanted to stay alive and in one piece it was now up to me to give the performance of a lifetime. It was a slim chance, but the only one I had.

'Well, what do you say?' Aleesh prompted me. 'What is your opinion of the Egyptian Intelligence Service?'

'My compliments, gentlemen,' I replied. 'An extremely neat job. Congratulations.'

Now I'd committed myself – but I was convinced it was the only possible way to play it.

The three of them beamed. 'Praise from you is praise indeed,' said Mahfous, 'let me return the compliment. You were the cleverest agent that ever operated in Egypt. Your cover was perfect. If it hadn't been for your wireless, which we finally located, you could have continued for another twenty years and nobody . . .'

'That's enough,' Aleesh interrupted him, 'we are not here to make small talk and exchange compliments. This is an interrogation.'

'It looks more like a tea party,' said Abdul Hakim grimly in Arabic, 'I am against this soft line. Give me two hours alone with this fellow and he will sing the most beautiful of songs for us.'

'He will in any case,' replied Aleesh. 'Let me try it my way for the time being. You may get your chance later, Abdul Hakim.' To me he said in English: 'Well, Mr Lotz, what is your decision? Will you cooperate?'

I shrugged. 'What other choice, have I? The game is up and I might as well tell you everything.'

'That would be very wise. You will not regret it. In the

end we will become good friends, you'll see. Have another
cigarette.'

'How did you manage to catch me out?' I asked casually,
lighting a cigarette. 'I mean, what put you on my track?
You said yourself my cover was perfect.'

Aleesh laughed loudly. 'Has your professional pride been
hurt? I'm afraid I can't tell you that, Mr Lotz. It is I who
will ask the questions, if you don't mind. Tell me this:
when was your code last changed?'

'About five months ago.'

'I see. And what happened to the previous codes, have
you still got them?'

'Of course not. They were destroyed. You don't imagine
I would keep them as souvenirs.'

'Hardly. Can you remember the contents of the previous
messages? I mean before the code was changed.'

'That was a long time ago. I can remember them in
general terms, but not every single message word for word,
naturally.'

'I see. We shall talk about the messages later. Now tell
me something about yourself. When were you born and
where?'

'On the sixth of January, nineteen-twenty-one in Mannheim, Germany. I grew up in Berlin.'

'Tell us about it. Did you remain in Berlin all your life?
Where did you go? What did you do?'

'When I finished high school the war broke out and
I served in the Wehrmacht. First in Germany, then
in the Afrika Korps. I was taken prisoner here in
Egypt.'

'You seem to make a habit of it. What rank did you
reach in the Wehrmacht?'

'Captain.'

'Only a Captain? I think you have told us your first lie,
Mr Lotz. Don't you want to reconsider your answer?'

'What is there to reconsider? What difference does it make

to my present position whether I was a Captain or a Field
Marshal. Rommel was running the show, not I.'

'I think you never served under Rommel. Isn't it true that
you held the rank of Colonel in the SS?' – Naturally they
had heard that story too. It might be to my advantage to
admit it eventually, but not now. Better let them get it out
of me the hard way, it would be more convincing.

'That is an unfounded rumour,' I responded. 'The truth
is that I was a Captain in the infantry. Why should I lie
about it?'

'I'll let it pass for the moment. What did you do after
the war?'

'I emigrated to Australia. At first I worked as a truck
driver, later I established myself as a horsebreeder.'

'And you became a millionaire?'

'That's the story I told, to explain my being able to spend
so much money. I managed to save up a small amount, but
spent most of it when I returned to Germany in fifty-
eight.'

'How did you come to work for Israel?'

'What makes you so sure I worked for Israel?'

'Come, Mr Lotz, don't try to play games with us. The
range of your transmitter and direction of your aerial prove
conclusively that you were transmitting to Israel. What made
you become a spy for them? Are you Jewish?'

'Certainly not. You only have to look to see I'm not
circumcised.'

'Don't worry, we will! But for the moment, answer my
question. What makes a former SS Colonel turn into a spy
for Israel? Money? Threats? Blackmail?

'Well, I was hard up. I like to live well, but couldn't
afford it. My salary as a riding instructor was quite small.
Then I met this Israeli who offered to buy me a horse farm
in Cairo and pay me a generous monthly salary in return
for a little information, things I heard and saw here. It
seemed quite simple. They taught me how to use a radio,

gave me a general idea of what they wanted, and a few weeks later I came over.'

'Someone will sit with you and get the exact details. How you were recruited, who trained you, what kind of training you underwent and where, what orders you received, who your contacts were, everything. Right now I only want a general outline to see how far you are willing to cooperate.'

There was a knock on the door and a guard entered. He went across to Aleesh and whispered into his ear. Aleesh got to his feet. 'I'm wanted upstairs,' he said, 'I need you too, Mahfous. Abdul Hakim, you carry on with Lotz, you know what to ask him. I shall have you relieved later.' He and Mahfous hurried out.

When we were alone, Abdul Hakim leaned back in his chair regarding me with a cynical smile. 'Now then, Mr Lotz,' he drawled, 'we shall carry on the good work.' He reached over and switched on the two projectors.

'Do you have to do that?' I asked. His smile widened into a sneer.

'Yes, of course,' he said, 'I can see you better this way. Does the light make you feel uncomfortable, hurt your eyes, perhaps? That's just too bad, Mr Lotz! This is an interrogation room, not a millionaire's villa. All considered, we're treating you pretty well. We can treat you quite differently, I assure you. This is not even a proper interrogation, just a friendly chat. But be careful, Lotz. Unless you are extremely cooperative in every way we shall employ other methods. I just thought I'd warn you. Are you ready to go on now, Mr Lotz?'

'What do you want to know?'

'Tell me about your wife? What part did she play in the spy ring?'

'There was no spy ring. I worked quite alone and my wife knew nothing.'

'Do you really expect me to believe that? I am not a complete fool. Do you mean to tell me that your wife knew absolutely nothing about your being a spy? What did you do with her when you were transmitting from your bedroom, lock her up?'

'She knew I was engaged in some political work, but no more than that. I had told her never to ask me questions about it.'

'And she had no part in it? A very likely story.'

'I was determined to keep her out of it. She wouldn't have liked it. It would have frightened her.'

'How thoughtful of you. How long have you been married?'

'Four years.'

'Do you love your wife, Mr Lotz?'

'Very much.'

'I know. That is the first true word you have said to me. How would you like it if I went to get the truth out of her? Perhaps beat her a little on the soles of her feet or put her into ice cold water for a while, let's say for twenty-four hours? Or gave her a few mild electric shocks... Now let's start again. Where did you first meet your wife?'

'I met her on a train between Paris and Munich. She had been in the United States, and had come to see her parents and have a holiday.'

'And when did you get married.'

'A few weeks later.'

'Now really, this is going a little too far. I would have expected a man of your intelligence to think up a more convincing story. Isn't it true that your wife, who is a trained agent, was supplied to you by the Israeli secret service because you needed an assistant? Isn't that a fact? Didn't she take an active part in all your operations?'

'She did not. Why can't you get that into your head! I don't deny that my wife was very useful to me in many ways because she blended perfectly with my cover, but that was coincidental. She was an excellent hostess to my many guests. She acted naturally because she had nothing to hide.

As for her being "supplied" to me as you put it, the very idea
is absurd. It is true that we met and got married under
somewhat unusual circumstances, but it is exactly this fact
which proves that I am not lying to you. Just think for a
moment. You said yourself that I could have thought up a
more convincing story. I certainly could and so could Israeli
intelligence. If she was an agent attached to me for duty,
she would have had a perfectly natural and convincing cover
story and all the documents to prove that we had been
married for ten or twelve years. Doesn't that make sense to
you?'

'She might have been planted on you without your knowledge.'

'That's most unlikely, impossible in fact. I would have
found out before long. As I said, she is much too naïve.
She would not have been able to deceive me for long.'

'Perhaps not. In that case it must have been done with
your knowledge and consent. I am not prepared to believe
your ridiculous tale about meeting her on a train and getting
married right away.'

'But it's true, I can tell you no more than that.'

'All right, let's start again at the beginning. What were
you doing in Paris just before you claim to have met your
wife?'

He made me relate the precise circumstances of our meeting. What exactly she had said to me and I to her? On whose
orders had I taken that particular train? What had she been
doing in the United States? Did I know any of her friends?
Why had her parents come to Egypt? It went on for hours
and hours until at last the door opened to let in Mahfous
and a guard. 'I am relieving you,' Mahfous said to Abdul
Hakim. 'Go and rest up for a while.' He switched off the
projectors and the guard placed a small plate of foule and
a glass of tea on the desk before me. 'Have some breakfast,
Mr Lotz,' said Mahfous, 'I have brought you some cigarettes
too.'

'Breakfast? What time is it?'

'Past nine.'

So we had been at it for at least nine hours. No wonder I was feeling sick and exhausted, my head not seeming to belong to me anymore. 'I can do with the tea and a cigarette,' I said, 'but I am too tired to eat anything.'

'No, no you must eat to keep up your strength. Do you want to freshen up?'

'Yes.' At a sign from him the guard placed a hood over my head and led me out of the room. After I had washed my face and neck under a tap and relieved myself, the hood was replaced and I was taken back to the interrogation room. Mahfous had seated himself behind the desk. He regarded me thoughtfully while I drank my tea and smoked a cigarette.

'Are you ready to go on now, Mr Lotz?' he asked me.

'Aren't you going to let me rest a bit?'

'I'm sorry, but we have to continue. You will rest later.'

He turned on the projectors again.

'At least keep these things out of my eyes,' I said.

'Unfortunately I can't do that. Orders. They will help you concentrate.'

'I don't find it so.'

'You will get used to them. Now, you were telling Abdul Hakim some stories we find very hard to believe.'

'What I told him was the absolute truth. The truth is sometimes harder to believe than a well-prepared lie.'

'Sometimes it is. I am hoping for your sake, Mr Lotz, that you were really telling the truth. You must realize we have ways and means of checking your statements.'

'Check all you want. I told you I was willing to co-operate but you are making it very hard for me.'

'Not really. Obviously we can't just take your word for anything you say. Give us proof of your cooperation. Tell me the names of your contacts here in Cairo.'

'What do you mean by contacts?'

'Accomplices, members of your ring. We know there were several.'

'You can't possibly know that, because there were none. You are an intelligence officer, aren't you acquainted with the methods of modern espionage? The ring system is obsolete because it is not safe, any book on the subject will tell you that.'

'Weren't Kiesow and his wife working with you? You were often together.'

'Which should be the best proof they were not working with me. Do you think I'd be so stupid as to be seen almost daily with an accomplice?'

'They have admitted it!'

'They have admitted nothing of the kind. They are good friends of mine who did not have the slightest inkling of what I was doing.'

'What about Youssef Ghorab? Didn't you recruit him into your ring?'

'For the hundredth time – there was no ring! Ghorab had no idea of my secret activities. He would have had me arrested if he suspected anything.'

'Then why did you give him so many presents? An electric mixer, a tape recorder, two radios, money, an operation for his daughter, there is a list as long as my arm. You must have spent many hundreds of pounds on him. Why? Your organization would not have paid for it unless they got something substantial in return. What was it?'

'He helped me in many ways as one helps a friend, but it was done in all innocence. He knew nothing.'

'One does not have to bribe a friend in order to enlist his help. I thought you said you were going to cooperate, Mr Lotz. I am waiting for you to start telling us the truth. Now come on, who were your contacts?'

The hours passed. Who were my contacts? What about all the Generals I knew? How much was I paying them? What others were there? Who were the Israelis who had trained me? To whom did I report in Europe and where? Which of them had I met in Egypt?

Summoning all my will-power I tried to keep a clear head, telling him the truth on some points which I knew could be verified, inventing plausible lies on others. The irony was that he swallowed most of my lies but did not believe me when I told him the exact truth.

Eventually the guard led me to an adjoining room where I was given some food. On my return to the interrogation room I found Hassan Aleesh talking to Mahfous.

'Ah, our friend Lotz,' he greeted me. 'I hear that you are giving us the benefit of your cooperation, but only to a certain extent. You must tell us everything you know. Until you do we must keep these lights on, I'm afraid.'

'But I've told you the whole truth, what else do you want?'

'Some of what you told us is true, some is not. Sit down, I want to hear for myself what you have to say, a summary of what you have told the investigators. First question: Who were your contacts here in Egypt?'

We went through the whole rigmarole once more. Same questions, same answers. Hours of it, the lights trained relentlessly on my face.

'All right,' he said at last, 'this will do for a beginning. I will now take you upstairs to meet a very important, high-ranking gentleman. If he asks you any questions, answer them truthfully.'

With the hood once again over my head I was taken up two flights of stairs. When the hood was removed I found myself in a large, elegantly furnished office opposite a thickset, bull-necked man of about forty-five with a round, balding head and the regulation moustache. Although we had never met I recognized him instantly. It was Salah Nasr, head of the Egyptian intelligence and security services. Fouad had once pointed him out to me in front of the

K

Hilton Hotel. Hassan Aleesh and Mahfous were standing to attention near the door.

'Good evening, Mr Lotz,' Salah Nasr greeted me, 'take a seat.' – Was it evening? I had lost all count of time. The heavy curtains in front of the window were drawn.

'May I say that I am glad to have you with us,' he said with an ironic smile, 'although I am not sure you reciprocate the sentiment. But I am told you have decided to do the sensible thing and cooperate.'

'It seems I have no alternative,' I replied. 'It is the only way I can improve my situation.'

'Very true, very true. I will propose a deal to you, Mr Lotz. Anything you say here will remain between us. The Prosecutor-General, who prepares the case against you, will not be told anything you reveal to us. Do you know who I am?'

'No.'

'Well, it doesn't matter. We are intelligence officers. What we are interested in is information. It would not help me in any way to see you hanged. What would I get out of it? Nothing! On the other hand, it would definitely be to my advantage to keep you alive and well so you can work for us. Not now perhaps, but later. Instead of hanging you will live, and very soon may be free again. We might keep you out of prison altogether. What you must do now is open your heart to us and tell us every single thing you know. None of it will reach the Prosecutor-General, I give you my word on it.'

The old trick! I wondered how stupid he thought I was.

'What do you say to my proposal?' he was asking.

'It makes sense,' I replied smoothly. 'You have my full cooperation.'

'Good. Tell me, Mr Lotz, just why did you work for Israel? What made you do it? Was it the famous German guilt complex for killing off a few Jews during the war? Did they infect you with their ideology about Zionism, the

Promised Land of the Jews, the small peaceful little country surrounded by hostile savages, all that rubbish? Did you feel you had to do something for them in order to right the wrong, to atone for the crimes committed by the German Nation?'

'They mentioned it, but they realized very soon that this kind of talk would not get them what they wanted. I was in this business for cash, not medals. I have enough of those from the Second World War. The days when I was willing to risk my neck for some high-sounding ideology are over. The only thing that counts in this world is what you have in your pocket.' I hoped I was not overdoing the mercenary approach, but he seemed quite satisfied with my answer.

'We know you must have received a considerable amount of money,' he said, 'but was there nothing else? No threats, no pressure?'

'Well no, not really. They hinted, of course, that if I ever betrayed them the consequences would be most unpleasant. Their arm reaches far. But there were no actual threats.'

'Are you sure there wasn't another inducement, apart from the money they paid you? A little blackmail perhaps, something to do with your past which they threatened to reveal?'

There it was again: Obersturmbannführer Lotz. I pretended to hesitate. Having them believe the story of my Nazi past would further conceal my Israeli identity and increase my chances of staying alive.

'How could they blackmail me?' I replied. 'They know nothing about me.'

'I don't quite believe that, Mr Lotz. We know better. Why don't you tell us the whole truth, it will only be to your advantage.

*   *   *

Time and again I was pressed for details of my associates – my bosses, the contact men I met in Europe. Since I had agreed to cooperate fully, I had to come up with some kind of an answer and decided that the best thing would be to give fictitious names – names like Joseph, Rudi, and others. But my interrogators were not satisfied simply with names. They wanted to know what these men looked like, what mannerisms, characteristics, etc., they had. Since the questions were thrown at me night and day during the long weeks of interrogation I had to beware of contradicting myself. To avoid doing so I chose actual people I had known years ago, but who had not the slightest connection with Israeli Intelligence. In this way I was always able to picture an actual person and to give detailed and consistent descriptions.

My wife, of course, had no way of knowing what I was telling my interrogators. Frightened that she might incriminate me, she decided to say absolutely nothing. Eventually her interrogators realized she was not going to talk and decided to risk bringing us together – so that I could 'make her see reason'. I promised my cooperation and was conducted, with the usual blindfold over my head, to an office on the first floor. Samir Nagy, the Prosecutor-General, was sitting at a large wooden desk, his clerk Hamdy at his side.

'Where is my wife?' I asked.

'All in good time,' Nagy replied slowly.

'First I want your personal assurance that she will tell us everything she knows.'

'She will tell you whatever little she knows.'

'Good. If she does I will let you meet her more often, perhaps every day. Otherwise you will not see her until the trial. Now, remember, you may speak only in English.'

He pressed a button on his desk and Waltraud was led in by a guard. When her blindfold was removed she gave a small cry and rushed into my arms. She still had on the same slacks and blouse she had been wearing on our trip to Mersa

Matrouh: an old coat of mine that had been lying in the back of the car hung over her shoulders. She was terribly pale, her face bruised and her hair dishevelled. We embraced warmly – much to the delight of the men in the room. Kissing a woman in public, even one's wife, was considered something of an obscenity in Egypt.

Hassan Aleesh interrupted us. 'When you have finished exchanging caresses, perhaps we can get to the point,' he said bitingly. Samir Nagy silenced him with a glance.

'Sit down both of you,' he ordered. 'I understand, Mrs Lotz, that your husband wishes to say something to you.'

'Yes, Waltraud, I do. These men tell me you have refused to make a statement. Is that true?'

'Of course it's true,' she exclaimed, 'they want me to admit all sorts of idiotic things, like your being the head of an Israeli spy ring. Do you want me to "confess" to things that aren't true?'

'No, of course not, darling, that would be madness. You know full well I was never connected with any ring, though there's no denying I've done certain things which aren't quite legal. I've admitted that much. I had no choice. They have all the proof they need. Of course, I never told you exactly what I was doing. I kept you deliberately in the dark. But you do know something about my work – in very general terms, of course.'

Waltraud, realizing now what I had told them and quick to take her cue, replied: 'Yes. I knew that much. But I thought it would help you if I kept quiet.'

'That was sweet of you, my darling, but such evasions won't help either of us. They have too much evidence.'

Samir Nagy cleared his throat. 'Mrs Lotz, are you now willing to make a frank statement of the facts?'

'Yes, but only if my husband stays here with me.'

'This is highly irregular,' interrupted Aleesh in Arabic, 'I agreed to this confrontation only because . . .'

'I suggest you stay out of this!' snapped Samir Nagy

sharply. 'I'll do this my way – and get some results for a change. Now, Mrs Lotz, tell us what you wish to say.'

Aleesh kicked back his chair and stormed from the room. Waltraud hesitated, looking at me for guidance, unsure how to begin. In fact she never did begin for it was I who dictated 'her' statement to Nagy – just something general to the effect that she was aware I was engaged in economic work of a secret nature, that she had sometimes seen my operating a transmitter in our bedroom, that she didn't know to whom I was transmitting or who my principals were. Nothing more.

To my amazement Samir seemed to accept the statement I had dictated for Waltraud and said smilingly: 'It's a beginning, anyway. You see, Mrs Lotz, we are not exerting any pressure. Everything is strictly legal. . . .'

'Strictly legal,' rasped Waltraud suddenly, her eyes blazing. 'You call it strictly legal to strip a woman when you interrogate her, to punch her in the stomach and kick her in the back, to keep her immersed in ice-cold water for an entire night. You call *that* legal!'

For a moment I was too stunned by Waltraud's words to speak. Then, rising to my feet and slamming the desk, I began to shout at Samir. I reminded him we were German citizens and that if he ever intended to bring our case to court he'd have to let the German Consul see us sooner or later.

'You'll find descriptions of your interrogation methods on the front pages of newspapers throughout the world,' I told him. 'Is that what you want?'

Samir was biting his lips, visibly shaken by the outburst. 'I'd no idea such things had taken place,' he said faintly. 'It won't happen again.'

Then, turning to Hamdy, he rasped in Arabic: 'Bring them some coffee. I must see Hassan about this, I told the fool not to play rough with them. The Presidency wants a big trial, we can't afford a scandal at this stage.'

I was to see a great deal of Samir Nagy over the next days. His experts had succeeded in decoding most of the messages I had transmitted or received and he cross-examined me ponderously about each one. The protocol he was compiling grew dramatically, though I seemed to be holding my own.

*   *   *

My servant, Osman, was kept in a cell not far from mine. For days on end he was beaten mercilessly. I could hear his screams for hours at a time, and tackled Hassan Aleesh about it when I next saw him.

'Why are you beating him?' I demanded. 'The man is entirely innocent; he knows absolutely nothing about my activities. Surely you can't believe I'd take an Egyptian servant into my confidence. Why don't you release him?'

'Oh, I know he's innocent,' Aleesh replied with a grin, 'but you see, I'm very angry with him. While you were away in Mersa Matrouh I came to conduct a search of your house . . . and this impertinent fellow tried to prevent me entering.'

Poor Osman was beaten for two weeks before they let him go.

At about noon on the twelfth day after our arrest, Hassan Aleesh threw open the door of my cell. Slapping me on the shoulder and smiling broadly, he wished me a very good morning.

'Would you like to come and have breakfast with me and your wife?' he asked. Naturally I agreed eagerly to the suggestion.

'Well put on a suit and a nice tie,' he said to me, 'this is Friday [the Moslem day of rest] and of course you must look your best when you are having breakfast with such a charming woman as your wife. One of the guards will take you into the garden as soon as you are ready.'

With that he left. I dressed hurriedly and was led into a small garden enclosed by a high wall, where I joined Waltraud and Aleesh for breakfast. It was an opulent affair, with eggs, cold meat, foule and tea. Aleesh soon came to the point.

'Mr Lotz,' he said, 'how would you like to appear with your wife on Egyptian television?'

'What for?' I asked rather astonished.

'It would make things a little easier for you,' he replied. 'The public, and incidentally the judges, would see that you are actually rather a nice couple and this might influence them in your favour.'

'I had not expected anything like this, I will have to think about it,' I replied.

'Yes by all means think about it,' he said, 'you have three minutes.'

The bit about influencing the public in my favour was a load of bull of course but I realised I might be able to use the broadcast for some other purpose. Egyptian television was monitored by Israeli Intelligence and it might be that I could slip in a word or two to let the boys know exactly what was taking place.

'All right,' I said to Aleesh. 'I agree.'

'Then let's go,' he said getting up.

He led us into a large room on the ground floor where television cameras and all the necessary equipment had already been set up. We were asked to sit down at a table decorated with some flowers and were introduced to the man who was to interview us. Coffee was brought, cigarettes lit, and the interview began.

We were asked a great many questions regarding our personal history, the kind of life we had lived in Egypt and, in very general terms, details of our espionage activities. I admitted that I had been a spy, a German mercenary, and stressed that my wife had known practically nothing about my secret operations. In the end he asked me how I felt about the whole thing now, how I was being treated and if there was any message I would like to give to people in Germany. I replied that of course I regretted my actions very much, that it was only now that I realized the harm I had done out of greed for money and that I was being extremely well treated. When it came to my message to the people of Germany, I saw my chance and said: 'If the Israelis must send spies to Egypt, let them use their own people and not recruit Germans for this job. I strongly advise anyone in Germany who considers taking on such a job to resist.'

The point was to convey to my colleagues in Israel that my German cover was still intact, and I later learned that Israeli Intelligence had indeed taken the hint, and had been able to direct their activities on my behalf accordingly.

A morning or two later, during one of my sessions with Samir Nagy, the telephone on his desk rasped, and I realized from the change of tone in his voice that something was up. Evidently I was wanted in Hassan Aleesh's office and was to be escorted there immediately.

Waiting with Hassan Aleesh was Salah Nasr, the Chief of Intelligence. Aleesh dismissed the guard and signalled me to take a seat. Salah Nasr regarded me sternly. 'Mr Lotz,' he intoned, 'I'm surprised to learn that you have not told us the whole truth yet. It seems your activities were far more extensive than we thought. These articles on the desk here, do you know what they are?'

'Time pencils,' I replied – it had certainly taken them a long time to find them.

'How did you know that? Are you an explosives expert?'

'I don't have to be. You forget I served in the army. Any infantry officer must have seen thousands of these.'

'What are they used for?'

'For timing the ignition of a charge of explosives.'

'Exactly. I take it you did not keep these pencils as a souvenir from the war. How did they come into your possession?'

'Into my possession? They're nothing to do with me.'

'But they are. They were in a plastic package, concealed in a special pocket at the bottom of your bathroom scales. Do you mean to tell me, Mr Lotz, that you knew nothing about them?'

I told him that this was indeed so and that I was as surprised as he was. The package, I went on, had been given to me in Munich by a man called Erwin, one of my contacts, who had told me to take it to Cairo and hand it over to someone who would call for it. A man by the name of Hubert. That man never turned up and so I had just kept it. I had no idea what was in it and must have had it for years.

Nasr and Aleesh went into a whispered consultation. I was able to overhear only fragments, words like 'different device', 'never used before' and 'best way to make him confess'. They seemed to reach a decision and Salah Nasr turned to me once more.

'I'm not certain yet whether to believe you', he said, 'further investigations will have to be made. Now tell me something else: Have you ever sent any letters to German experts here in Egypt?'

'Yes, when I was in Europe I often sent letters and postcards to some of my friends in Cairo.'

'You know that is not what I mean. Some of the top experts received envelopes which exploded when they were opened, injuring them. Others were sent letters threatening them with injury or death if they did not give up their jobs and leave the country. I want you to tell me who sent those letters.'

'I'm sorry, this sort of thing was not in my line of work

at all; you must realize that, surely. I'm afraid I can't help you.'

They then went on to propose a deal, saying they would release Waltraud's parents if I signed a statement admitting that I had sent threatening letters and explosives to the German experts. At first I refused, protesting that since Waltraud's parents were quite innocent they would have to release them sooner or later anyway.

'I wouldn't count on that if I were you, Lotz. We could easily make up a case against them if necessary. Your father-in-law could also die of natural causes – he is a sick man. Or they could both be killed in a regrettable car accident on their way to the airport. Any number of things could happen.'

I was fairly sure he was bluffing and trying to intimidate me into signing, but could I take the chance of calling his bluff? My father-in-law was indeed a sick man: he had severe heart trouble and if he had to take much more of this, there was no telling what might happen to him.

'What exactly do you want me to sign?' I asked Nasr, after pausing to think for some minutes.

'I want you to write down a statement in English, in your own handwriting, saying that you sent threatening letters, some containing explosives, to certain German scientists and engineers by order of the Israeli Intelligence.'

'And you don't care whether this statement is true or not?'

'It's true all right. But that's not my concern. I want it only for my records. No one else will see it. Now, will you sign?'

'I'll tell you what I'm prepared to do – and mind you I'm doing it under extreme pressure – I'll admit that I had orders to send a number of threatening letters, but that I did not know some of them contained explosives until I heard about it from the recipients themselves.'

'All right, do it like that if you want. You did know, you

did not know, what difference does it make? What matters is that you admit sending them. You amuse me with your talk about "extreme pressures". You don't even know what pressure is. Three minutes of Abdul Hakim with a red-hot iron and you would have begged for permission to sign any kind of statement we wanted. You are lucky I am kindly disposed towards you, my dear Lotz. Now sign. It's only a formality, for my records. You have my word that the prosecutor will not be informed . . .'

Half an hour later I was back in Samir Nagy's office. He beamed at me as I entered.

'Come in, come in, Lotz, sit down. We can continue our conversation where we left off. But first let me order some coffee, you look tired. Rest and relax. Later you must tell me all about those explosives you sent to the German experts.'

*   *   *

The interrogation lasted for thirty-three days. Once it was over and it had been decided to hold a public show trial, orders were given to treat us particularly well and to grant us all possible privileges. I was transferred to Kanater prison, and had been there only a day when I was informed by the warder, Sergeant-Major Mohammad Battal, that my lawyers awaited me in the director's office. This was the first I'd heard about lawyers.

The prison director, General Khorollos, introduced me to two men. One was an Egyptian called Ali Mansour. Mansour told me that he did a great deal of work for the German Consulate in Cairo and that they'd appointed him my defence counsel. Bowing, scraping and smiling, he assured me that he was one of the best barristers in Egypt, that he was my friend and that I could safely leave my affairs in his capable hands.

The other man was a German in his mid-fifties, tall, slim,

and with greying blond hair. He clicked his heels in the
typical manner of a former German army officer, bowed
from the waist and told me in a clipped, military voice that
his name was Hans Peter Krahl-Urban. He explained that
my former comrades in the war had retained him. According to the tradition of the German army, he went on, they
would stand by me now, come what may, and indeed had
already raised a sum of money for my immediate needs.
Since I had never served in the German army I had a fairly
good idea who had sent him.

A few minutes later Waltraud was led into the room by a
policewoman, and the two lawyers were presented. I signalled to her with my eyes, and she understood immediately,
seating herself next to the Egyptian lawyer and engaging him
in conversation. I sat at the other side of the room next to
Krahl-Urban, who asked me in the same clipped accent
about prison conditions and the like, adding in an undertone, 'Greetings from . . .' (mentioning the name of one of
my close associates). Krahl-Urban explained that he had come
for just a few days, to make sure I had everything I needed
and was being well-treated, and that he would return to
Egypt before the trial started. As a German he was not
permitted to plead in an Egyptian court and could act only
as observer and adviser to my Egyptian defence counsel, Ali
Mansour. I gladly agreed to leave my affairs in his hands.

10

The Honourable Court

Our trial lasted from July 27, 1965 until August 21. As far as security precautions went, Samir Nagy was certainly leaving nothing to chance. Fifteen officers and eighty heavily armed policemen had been detailed to accompany us on our daily trip from Kanater prison to court and back. Road blocks had been set up in the vicinity of the courtroom building and machine guns were posted on the roofs of adjoining houses. Surrounding the building itself, several hundred policemen stood shoulder to shoulder, rifles and bayonets at the ready. A brigadier-general, perspiring with excitement, was in command of the whole operation. It was the time-honoured Egyptian method of grossly overdoing things once official minds were made up that they had to be done.

At the first session of the court, which lasted only ten minutes and was held for the purpose of postponing the trial for a month, the place had resembled a film studio rather than a courtroom. The president of the court, Hassan El-Badawy, had sternly reminded the television teams that they would have to restrain themselves at all future hearings. Even so, a barrage of flashlights confronted us as the trial finally got under way.

I faced ten charges, each of which carried the death sentence.

The charges were:

1 Conspiring to commit acts of espionage for an enemy country.

2 Continuously committing acts of espionage for an enemy country.

3 Conspiring to undermine the security of the United Arab Republic and its armed forces.

4 Continously committing acts with the object of undermining the security of the United Arab Republic and its armed forces.

5 Committing unlawful acts by order and for the benefit of a country with which the United Arab Republic was at war.

6 Being in unlawful possession of dangerous explosive materials.

7 Despatching threatening letters to foreign nationals employed by the Government of the United Arab Republic.

8 Despatching letters containing dangerous explosives to foreign nationals employed by the Government of the United Arab Republic.

9 Causing severe bodily harm to foreign nationals employed by the Government of the United Arab Republic as well as to citizens of the United Arab Republic.

10 Attempting to kill foreign nationals employed by the Government of the United Arab Republic as well as citizens of the United Arab Republic by means of dangerous explosives.

On trial with us was our close friend Franz Kiesow, the Cairo representative of the huge German industrial concern of Mannesmann. He and his wife Nadia were among the many Germans and Egyptians (numbering about a hundred and twenty) who'd been detained and interrogated immediately after our arrest – all people who had been our friends in Cairo, or who had maintained social contact with us in some way.

Kiesow's wife, Nadia, had been released after a month of fruitless third degree, but Franz himself stood accused of undermining state security. The secret police had found in his flat copies of reports he had sent to his firm in Germany – reports which gave a fairly clear picture of the deteriorating economic situation in the United Arab Republic: although these were quite accurate they were considered detrimental to the Egyptian economy. The actual evidence against Kiesow was flimsy, even by Egyptian standards, and his flock of German lawyers, provided by his firm, were later able to prove that all the information contained in his reports had appeared at some time or other in either the European or American press.

I had expected the prosecution to present its case to begin with, and was therefore surprised when the president opened the proceedings by calling me to the witness stand. An interpreter had been provided, but after it turned out that this gentleman's knowledge of the German language was quite insufficient, the president offered to hear my evidence in English, which he himself spoke well.

'Have you received a copy of the charge sheet and have you read and understood the charges preferred against you?', he began his questioning.*

'Yes, Your Honour.'

'How do you plead to the charges, guilty or not guilty?'

'I plead guilty to the first six charges and not guilty to the other four.'

The words were hardly out of my mouth when half a dozen reporters jumped from their seats and ran out to the nearest telephones. When order was restored the hearing continued. The questions were the same as in Samir Nagy's

* I would emphasize here that the excerpts from the court proceedings, including the prosecution's summing up, are taken from an actual transcript of the trial.

carefully prepared protocol and so, needless to say, were
my answers. After weeks of rehearsing them with Samir I
knew them by heart. Whenever my answer deviated in the
slightest from what I had said previously, the president
would raise his eyebrows in astonishment, saying 'but during
the interrogation you stated...', and I would rectify the
error. Names of Egyptian officers were not mentioned, as
had been agreed previously. The one exception was Youssef
Ghorab, whose sudden removal from the post of governor
and expulsion from the police force had caused much public
comment. My wireless communication equipment was produced and I was asked to demonstrate its operation and
explain to the court the system of coding messages. After
four hours of this the court was adjourned until the following day. That was when the fun started. Again I was called
to the stand and the questioning continued more or less in
the same vein. They wanted a general outline of my work:
'No details, please. Just answer the questions of the court.
We shall soon retire into secret session and hear further
evidence which is not for publication.'

At this point Samir Nagy rose, waving a document.

'Before we go into secret session, Your Honour, I would
like to submit this in evidence.'

'Go ahead, Samir.'

'Your Honour, a letter has reached me from Germany,
written by a person whose identity I cannot reveal in public.
The letter concerns the accused Wolfgang Lotz and I shall
read to the court an Arabic translation of the German
original:

> To the Prosecutor General: July 12, 1965
> A few weeks ago we discussed with Professor Pilz* the

---

* Pilz and his group of scientists had begun their activities at the rocket
station of Peenemunde, assisting internationally famous experts like Werner
von Braun and General Bornberger to produce Hitler's V-1 and V-2
rockets. They were now employed by the Egyptians, trying to produce
ground-to-ground missiles for use against Israel.

L

Lotz case and I am now informtd that in addition to his German nationality, Lotz also holds Israeli
nationality. According to my information Lotz was
born in Mannheim in 1921. In 1933 he emigrated to
Palestine with his mother and after the establishment
of the State of Israel in 1948 he acquired Israeli
nationality. I was also informed that he served as an
officer in the Israeli army. These details are also known
to the German authorities and I was informed that a
senior Israeli official arrived in Hamburg a few days
ago in order to try to prevent this information from
being published in a German magazine.*

The object is to hide Lotz's past and, yet more important, his Israeli nationality. It is possible that these
facts are already known to you but I feel it my duty
to point them out again so that Lotz can be made to
reveal the identity of the people who sent explosives
from Germany to Dr Pilz's secretary and a number
of Egyptians.

Yours very truly. . . .

Seating himself, Samir folded his arms across his belly
and regarded me with a triumphant smirk. There was a
commotion in the audience and the reporters began scrib-
bling frantically. Another sensation for their front pages.
Waltraud paled and seemed close to tears. 'Try not to look
so frightened,' I told her, forcing myself to smile. 'If they
believe any of this, it's the end.'

Krahl-Urban, my German lawyer, apparently held the
same opinion. His face was grave and he was talking urgently
to Ali Mansour, our defence counsel.

Mansour rose to address the court. 'Your Honour,' he
said, 'this is not evidence. This is hearsay. If the prosecution

* Der Stern's ace reporter Wolfgang Löhde had indeed unearthed the
true facts of my past. Fortunately for me the chief editor agreed to hold
back the story in order to save my life.

wants to submit this letter in evidence, the author of the letter must appear in person before this court and be sworn in. I move to disregard this doubtful document.'

'It is perhaps not properly presented,' replied the president, 'however the court wishes to question the accused on this point. Mr Lotz, have you understood the text of this letter?'

'Not quite, Your Honour, I'm afraid my Arabic is not good enough for that. May I see the German original?'

'Yes, you may approach the bench and read it.'

'But not the signature, Your Honour! I promised my informant absolute secrecy,' cried Samir Nagy.

'All right.' The president folded back the bottom part of the letter, so that the signature could not be seen, and handed it to me. There was no need for me to try and see the signature. A letterhead two inches high adorned the top of the page: 'Dr Alfred Seidl, Attorney-at-Law, Munich.' Address and telephone number were also given. I knew Seidl to be the legal adviser of the Pilz group, the rocket experts. This was a noble effort on the part of those merchants of death to get me hanged.

'What do you have to say about this letter, Mr Lotz?'

'It's absolute nonsense, Your Honour. Vicious nonsense. The only true part about these preposterous allegations is the fact that I was born in Mannheim on the date mentioned. Otherwise there is not a word of truth in them.'

'Did you ever go to Israel?'

'Yes, Your Honour.'

'Tell the court a few more details.

'I went to Israel only once and stayed there for just six days. That was at the beginning of 1963. I had gone to Paris on one of my regular routine visits and met Joseph as usual. He told me the organization had decided I should go to Israel for a few days, that the visit should be absolutely secret and that a high ranking personality in Israel wanted to meet me. So I flew to Israel. On my first day there I travelled round a bit, accompanied by a man called Rudi.

On my second day I met a man named Meyer. Rudi had told me that he was a very high ranking personage. We had dinner together and he asked me a great many questions about Egypt. He also asked me details about my cover and about the type of information I was gathering for Israel's intelligence and the methods I employed to gain the information. He also wanted to know my general impressions of Egypt and if I was feeling safe and secure in my cover. He complimented me on my achievements.'

'What did you do during the other four days?'

'I went with Rudi on several trips round the country.'

'Did you visit Haifa?'

'Yes, but only briefly.'

'Did you acquire Israeli nationality while you were there?'

'Certainly not. As I told you before, my visit lasted only a few days.'

'What is your opinion about this letter?'

'Everything the letter says is an absolute lie. As I've already said, the only true fact is that I was indeed born in Mannheim, Germany in 1921. The writer or writers only want to harm me. I have a fair idea who they might be.'

'In that case we shall retire into secret session and you may tell us about your suspicion.'

On the way to the judge's chambers I was stopped by Ali Mansour. 'I want to speak to you about the letter before we go in,' he said.

'Yes. Listen, Mansour, I don't have to tell you how dangerous this letter is. You must convince the court that it's a pack of lies.'

'Of course, of course, I'll do that, don't worry. But I, as your lawyer must know the real facts. It's true, isn't it, what the letter says?' – The double-faced bastard! What a friend Samir Nagy had in this crook!

'The letter is a lie from beginning to end,' I said vehemently.

'You are an Israeli though, aren't you?'

'I am *not*, blast you, and you know it!'

'But your mother is Jewish. Where does she live, in Tel-Aviv?'

'Both my parents were killed in an air raid in Berlin in 1944. My mother was a Protestant. Where do you get all these stupid ideas? You are worse than the prosecutor. Perhaps I'd better get myself another lawyer.'

'Come, Mr Lotz, don't excite yourself. I only want the best for you.'

'The best? You haven't even found time to discuss my defence with me.'

'Your defence is well prepared. Things are not done here as they are in Germany. Trust me, Mr Lotz, I'm your friend. We must go in now, the judges are waiting.'

The three judges and Samir were seated in shirt sleeves at a large oblong table. Ali Mansour and I were invited to join them and to take off our jackets and ties, which was a relief in the oppressive heat of the Egyptian summer. My escort, Major Farid, took a seat near the door. Coffee and cold lemonade were served, cigarettes lit and the gathering began to look more like a tea party than a court of law. Samir greeted me with a wide smile and outstretched arms. 'I hope you're not angry, Mr Lotz. About the letter I mean. I was only doing my job. In a courtroom one sometimes has to use theatrical effects, you know.'

'You went a little too far,' I said, accepting a cigarette from the president. 'It will be a nice theatrical effect if the judges believe this rubbish. Really, Samir, that was too much and it wasn't in the script either.'

Hassan El-Badawy laughed. 'I hear you and Samir have become quite good friends,' he said.

'Friends or not, this is a lousy joke to play on anybody, Your Honour. If you give me time I can prove none of this is true.

'Relax, Mr Lotz, we know perfectly well the letter is a – what shall we call it – a frame-up. You see, we've made a study of your personal history and we know all about you, practically from the day you were born. There are certain parts of your past which you are trying to conceal, but being an Israeli officer does not fit into our picture of you. The court will disregard the letter and not admit this clumsy falsification as evidence. Mr Lotz, who do you imagine would do a thing like that and for what reasons?'

'It is clearly an attempt to get me executed,' I replied, 'and the only people who would gain anything from it are the Pilz group and the Jews. The Pilz group are after revenge because I made fools of them and they believe I had something to do with sending them explosive parcels, which I did not. The Israelis on the other hand might want to eliminate an agent for whom they have no further use and who is now cooperating with the Egyptian authorities. Those are the only explanations I can think of.'

'You might be right, Mr Lotz. This is a very dirty business and we shall say no more about it. We shall now continue to hear evidence which is not to be made public.'

In an informal manner he asked me about Egyptian officers and officials whom I had used as sources of information. I answered automatically, sticking to the text of the protocol. Everything was back to normal, so to speak, and the unpleasant sensation of a noose about to encircle my neck gradually disappeared.

'This concludes your evidence,' said the president after half an hour, 'tomorrow we shall call your wife to the witness stand. The court will adjourn until tomorrow.'

Early next morning, before the guards came to take me to court, the prison nabatchy, who was in charge of newspapers and mail and had become friendly with me, entered my cell. He was very agitated, flung a newspaper down on to the bed and asked me:

'Are you an Israeli?'

'What gives you that ridiculous idea?' I replied.

Picking up the newspaper he began to read from the
printed page:

'It is known that Israeli intelligence is now trying fever-
ishly to support the German spy Lotz. This is in spite
of the fact that he has made a full confession and disclosed all the secrets of the espionage and terror ring
which he headed. The Israeli purchasing mission in
Cologne, West Germany, which is in fact a cover for
a branch of the Israeli Secret Service, is now engaged
in some frantic activity. The deputy director of the
mission, who is an Israeli intelligence officer, went
to see the chief editor of the German weekly *Der
Stern* in order to prevent publication of the greatest
sensation in the Lotz story, namely the fact that he emigrated to Palestine with his mother in 1933 and lived
there until 1948 when the State of Israel was established. Later Lotz served for many years as a commis-
sioned officer in the Israeli army. For a month the
German weekly had a sensational article ready which
they intended to publish during the trial, under the title
'That *is what Lotz said* – This *is the truth.*' Why does
Israeli intelligence act in this fashion? Are they afraid
that the disclosure of Lotz's real identity will result in
a fuller and more dangerous confession than that which
he had made until now? Is Lotz really an Israeli?

'Several Germans here have remarked on one fact regarding the languages Lotz speaks. He does not speak
German with the accent of the Rheinland where he
was born and his English is also not the English of a
German. It can therefore be assumed that he has lived
for many years outside Germany whereas he claims to
have been a German officer and that he later worked
in a riding school in Berlin, where the Israeli intelligence
found him. Most high ranking Nazis did not stay in
Germany after the war. All dangerous Nazis who remained in Germany after the war were either tried

and convicted or else committed suicide. If Lotz had been a Nazi he would have gone into hiding in some far country, as others did. If in spite of this he had remained in Germany and the Israeli intelligence had discovered him, they would have pressured and black-mailed him into working for them right there, serving Israel's aims in Germany itself. On the other hand, if Lotz had been an ordinary German army officer, as he has claimed, why leave Germany at all? He could have stayed and got an excellent and well paid post in Germany. And there are many other questions: Why is it that Lotz made such tremendous efforts to clear his wife and his friend Kiesow?

To have the kind of standing in the organization that Lotz clearly had, you must be an important member and also possess the nationality of the state you are working for.

It is logical that the standing of Lotz, the Israeli citizen who spied for Israel, is entirely different from the stand-ing of Lotz the German citizen who spied for Israel. It is natural that he now adopts the cover of a German who spied for Israel for the sake of money, taking into account the state of war which exists between Egypt and Israel. The new Israeli chief of intelligence does not wish his secret operations against Egyptian and German scientists in Egypt to become public know-ledge, and the letter which the Prosecutor General had received from Germany contains hints regarding this.'

Coming on top of the letter that had been read out in court the previous day, this article made my situation pre-carious, and the minute I got into the court-room I dis-cussed it with Krahl-Urban, who in turn conferred with Ali Mansour. As soon as the court session began, Ali Mansour jumped to his feet requesting permission to speak on a matter of urgency.

'Your Honour,' he began, 'I have here a newspaper article published this morning; it is full of conjectures and distortions and serves only to bias the court and public opinion against the accused. Egyptian law guarantees every accused a fair trial – by the court and not by the press.'

'Yes,' replied the president of the court, 'I've read the article myself and I hereby warn the press that if they do not confine themselves to reporting the actual proceedings of this court they will be banned from the hearing.'

I was somewhat relieved, but still a little puzzled by their eagerness to avoid the whole question of my possible Israeli identity. Surely the possibility of my being an Israeli must have occurred to them, even before the trial: after all, I had been interrogated for thirty-three days. They were of course not very logical thinkers, but they were by no means fools. Even the best of covers contained weak links – and mine was no exception. Any thorough investigation would have at least raised some doubts and exposed certain facts that were not in keeping with the general picture of myself, my past and my activities that I presented them with; yet both the president of the court and the prosecutor general had readily accepted my explanation concerning the letter and had also disregarded the article.

Why had they agreed so readily to drop the subject of the letter? There could be several explanations. One was that they actually believed my story. After all I had been 'identified' as a former SS colonel and although I had denied the story everybody still believed it. Another possible explanation was that they suspected the truth but that because relations between Egypt and West Germany were extremely strained, it suited them to have German and not Israeli scapegoats to give them yet another reason for breaking off diplomatic relations with West Germany. The third possibility was this: I had worked in Egypt for five years without anybody suspecting me. I had been arrested and interrogated. The prosecutor general had written a protocol of over 1,800 folio pages about the confessions and activities of the German called Lotz: then suddenly the anonymous letter arrived. It might have been too shameful for the Egyptian authorities to admit that an Israeli intelligence officer had hoodwinked them and collected extremely valuable military and other information over a period of five years. Furthermore, that he had succeeded in deluding the court and the prosecution. It was possible that the Egyptians, who have a very delicate sense of prestige, often bordering on the ridiculous, simply could not admit, even to themselves, that the facts about my Israeli identity were indeed true.

Waltraud was now called to the stand. It was a repeat performance of my own testimony and over in a couple of hours. She had had only an inkling of what I had been doing, and apart from the fact that on occasions she had seen me transmit and receive wireless messages, she had known practically nothing. Yes, she was aware that I had often invited people to my home for the purpose of acquiring information and she had done her best to create a suitable atmosphere at these parties. No, she had not known what kind of information I was after. She had been a housewife, no more.

'Now that you have heard what your husband was doing, what is your opinion of him?' asked the president of the court.

'Naturally I was rather shocked when I heard about it, but a wife must stand by her husband in times of misfortune. Strange as it may seem to you, I love my husband more than ever now. His fate is in your hands and I appeal to the court not to be too severe on him. It is my hope that one day we shall be free and together again, to live in peace in some remote corner of the world where nobody knows us.'

'A good try,' I said to her when she returned from the witness stand. Nevertheless, the chances of her hopes coming true seemed rather dim at that moment.

Kiesow, the third accused, was called next. He answered a few routine questions regarding his personal status and then the court retired into secret session for a whole day. The public was not to learn the contents of his reports, which gave the true facts about the economic situation in Egypt.

For another three days a variety of witnesses were presented. A signal officer explained the range and method of operation of my transmitter. A coding expert testified to having decoded my messages. Another officer produced the explosives found in my possession and some others I had never seen before. Finally, a postmaster testified to having lost an eye when a letter addressed to one of the German scientists exploded in his hand. He omitted to explain why the letter had been opened by him in the first place. (The mail of foreign experts working in Egypt was of course carefully censored).

For the appearance of the next witness the courtroom was cleared of spectators and newsmen. A dapper army major marched in, came to attention in the witness stand and saluted the court smartly.

'What appointment do you hold, Major?' asked the president after the man had given his name.

'I am here as a representative of the Ministry of War, Your Honour.'

'What evidence can you give in this case?'

'I was given the assignment of reading and analyzing the information contained in the wireless messages sent by the accused Wolfgang Lotz.'

'What did the messages say?'

'Most of them contained secret or top secret information on military or political subjects. It was my job to evaluate those items of information which were of a military nature.'

'Were they correct? How far did they conform with the facts?'

'After a most careful examination the Ministry of War came to the conclusion that ninety-six per cent of the information transmitted by the accused was correct, Your Honour.'

'How high do you assess the actual or potential damage this information has done to the United Arab Republic?'

'That is hard to estimate precisely, Your Honour.'

'Would you say the damage was considerable?'

'Very considerable, Your Honour.'

'Thank you, Major, that will be all.'

I turned to Waltraud in despair: 'Why doesn't that idiot Mansour cross-examine any of the witnesses?'

Her reply was fast: 'What do you want him to do, knock off two per cent? I think ninety-six is pretty good. Let anyone try and beat that.'

When the witness steppped down the president turned to the prosecutor. 'Will there be any more witnesses today, Mr Samir?' 'No, Your Honour. With your permission I shall begin to sum up the case for the prosecution tomorrow morning.'

'What about the German witnesses that appear on your list?' 'They will not be here to testify, Your Honour. All three of them have written to me from Germany to say that the pressure of business prevents them from coming to Egypt in the near future.'

'Then we shall have to do without them. The court is adjourned until nine o'clock tomorrow morning.'

*   *   *

The prosecution's summing-up took two days. With all the oriental oratory at his command, and underscoring his arguments with a wealth of theatrical gestures that even drew an occasional smile from the bench, Samir Nagy began his flowery and impassioned speech:

'Your honour the president, honourable councillors. From the heights of treason, from the summit of treachery and from the darkness of debasement, we have brought these three accused, the like of whom we have yet to find in our history. A very long time will pass before we shall find again, if ever, such a master of deception and treachery. Israeli Zionism could find no better servant than Lotz, their chief butcher. The heads of Israeli intelligence even invited Lotz, the master of treachery, to visit Israel in January 1964 in order to celebrate with him and congratulate him. The master accepted the invitation and in Tel-Aviv he met their highest leader, Mayer, and had dinner with him. This high honour was not bestowed on him for nothing. It was to show their appreciation of his efforts and operational efficiency; he was also rewarded with considerable amounts of money.

'Another miracle concerning the sorcerer was his deep insight into human character. Whenever he met one of his victims he started looking for the weak points in his character. For example, he described a certain man, and his weakness for women and proposed: "The next time he goes to Vienna I suggest that a woman should be supplied in order to extract important information from him." He is indeed a genius of deception and a master of corruption. He struck up a close friendship with one of the German scientists and immediately began reporting all the information this man gave him in his unsuspecting innocence. The wireless transmitter was kept busy with plans of treason and murder. This innocent scientist told Lotz that he suspected a certain woman to be a spy. The name of this woman is Caroline Bolter. She was a member of Lotz's spy ring and ordered to spy on this particular German expert. When she became suspect, Lotz immediately sent a wireless message asking for her removal. Caroline Bolter was removed from Egypt the very next day.

'Not enough blood had this murderer spilled, but he continued to ask for additional destructive materials in order to carry on with his murderous schemes. In his message No.

9, he said. "The letter which was sent to Kirmeir did not explode. Another letter did explode in the Meadi post office. This made a strong impression on the German scientists."

'In his message No. 20 he says: "A number of scientists employed in Helwan have submitted their resignations, others will leave in the spring and new ones will arrive within the next few months. I will try to take them in hand." In yet another message he says: "I am sure we can induce additional German scientists to leave by dispatching more threatening letters and by seeing that they are published in the German press." All this he did to his own kind and to his own countrymen assisted by his wife, that striped poisonous snake, and without the slightest feeling of mercy. Just for their hobby of adventurism and to satisfy their greed for money.

'During the interrogation Lotz even admitted this frankly and I was shocked to hear him say it. I asked him, "Why did you agree to do all this?" and he replied, "It was my job, just as it is your job to sit there and ask me questions." As it is written in The Protocols of the Elders of Zion, "The passport to this world is falsehood, lies, exploitation of passion and prostitution."

'As for the third accused Kiesow I will say this: His sympathies lie with Israel. They lie with it to such an extent that Lotz said: "I did once consider recruiting him into the organization but I finally decided not to accept this responsibility because of his Egyptian wife who is a gossip. I therefore contented myself with the information Kiesow continuously supplied." The picture of Kiesow which Lotz drew for the organization appeared to them very satisfactory and Joseph, the head of the organization, asked Lotz to keep in close contact with Kiesow and continue receiving information from him.

'Those are the three accused persons whom I have mentioned now all in one breath. I will proceed to speak about them in more detail:

'In his so-called full confession, Lotz did not admit all his crimes in the beginning as he has claimed before this court. Only when he was confronted with the irrefutable evidence of his wireless transmitter hidden in the bathroom scales did he admit that he had this transmitter in his possession. He did not admit, he did not mention at the time, that there were also explosives hidden in the scales. Only when it became obvious to him that we were searching further and were about to discover the explosives did he admit possession of them. It was the same with the letters that contained explosives. In the beginning, Lotz claimed stubbornly that these were ordinary threatening letters. After he was softened up he had to admit the possibility of some of those letters containing explosives and finally he remembered we had intercepted his messages and deciphered the message where he asked for additional explosives.

'All of his many crimes were committed by order for a country with which Egypt is in a state of war and for that country's benefit. In his evidence before this court, the accused Lotz told us at great length about the fact that his wife knew little, if anything, about his activities and that her only role was that of a housewife and hostess to his many guests and that she innocently provided the perfect background for his cover as a rich horse-breeder.

'For many years I have been dealing with cases of espionage and I want to point out that in the Secret Service everything like marriage, divorce, pregnancy, love and hate is according to plan and by order. There is no marriage among agents except by approval of higher authority and there is no love except by order. Everything takes place under the supervision of the spy masters, including the wedding night, including unfaithfulness to one's spouse. And this has been proved in previous big spy trials.

'The last one was that of John Leon Thomas and his wife Kitty. Thomas, who had spied for Israel, was executed and his wife was also sentenced to death in her absence. It is interesting to note that the behaviour of Thomas during his trial was very similar to that of Lotz. The same story, the same web of lies, the same chance meeting in a railway compartment. John Leon Thomas was caught on January 5, 1961. Lotz arrived in Egypt two days later on January 7th. This could not possibly be a coincidence. What Lotz said about his wife is exactly what he had to say according to instructions. In other words he says, If I am caught, I shall try to clear my wife so that she can carry on with her part of the job.

'The Israeli spy organization agreed to Lotz's marriage and opened an account for her in a German bank for the sum of $15,000. The accused admitted during interrogation that his wife knew about his secret wireless transmissions and was witness to them. In fact her activities went far beyond those of an ordinary housewife. Remember how she stood guard outside his bedroom door while he was transmitting and how she accompanied him on his various journeys with the object of observing military instalments, how she invented a brain tumour in order to have an excuse to go abroad every six months, how she helped him gather information about secret rocket sites, about military airports and airfields, about new roads and daily reports of the war in Yemen, the German experts and the military industry.

'Here before you stand people who have lost all sense of human decency. Here before you stands a hired killer who has betrayed his own country and who admits himself that he has no interests except money. He said to me, "I do not work for medals, I got enough of those in the war, I do not suffer from the famous German guilt complex, I do not care for anything except money and my own pleasure."

'How, I ask you, can one have even the slightest degree of mercy for a man like that. How can one even begin to understand or justify in any way the motives that drove this man to espionage. Did not this country receive him in friendship and honour him, not suspecting the harm he was causing? And he proved his gratitude for the friendship and honours he had received here – with explosives. Ordinarily one could find in one's heart a certain degree of mercy, even for an enemy of the state, if there was one shred of decency left in him, and for this woman who makes such a great show of loving her husband. She loves him in spite of his crimes, in spite of his treachery, in spite of his baseness. What kind of love is this which is not beautiful but dirty? How can one describe her feeling for him as love, when it is nothing but cheap passion? What conscience can she have when she loves him in spite of all his dirty deeds? Her black soul was looking for a mate and darkness joined darkness. Now that they are asking for mercy, remind them of those whom they have deprived of life, hope and happiness. I am asking you to impose the maximum punishment on them and sentence them to death by hanging. For the sake of the eyes that can no longer see and for the sake of protecting our Holy Fatherland, I am asking you this in the name of the country whose sons you are, in the name of the country that raised you and made you what you are. As for those who sent these criminals to our country, their day will come. One day there will be trials in Tel-Aviv like the Nuremberg trials, where the enemies of humanity were convicted. I am not a dreamer and these are not figments of my imagination. I say that the Tel-Aviv trials will come. Historical justice will be done and I pray that we shall all live to see it.'

Before the court was adjourned the president announced that counsels for the defence would also be allowed two days to make their plea. On our way out, Samir smiled at us. 'See you in the morning,' he said, 'I wish you good luck!'

Waltraud shook her head in amazement. 'I shall never understand Egyptians,' she said.

M

Ali Mansour began his speech for the defence with an apology. 'I stand before this honourable court as the defence counsel of a foreign spy and his wife. He is a man who has done harm to our beloved motherland and who deserves to be punished. Naturally all of us turn away in horror from such a person, but by law he has the right to be defended in court by a lawyer. An Egyptian lawyer, a son of our people. The greatness and justice of our laws are borne out by the fact that they command us to defend even the lowest of criminals. Whatever my own feelings, I am here to do my duty.'

There was more of this, and it took him the best part of an hour to come to the point. I had confessed, he said, to six of the ten charges. The other four were baseless and the evidence inconclusive. He was not asserting that I was innocent – far from it – but the crimes I had in fact committed weighed heavily enough without adding others of which I was not guilty. The court had to take into consideration the mitigating circumstances of the case. The Second World War had broken off my career as a German officer and left me penniless and stranded. I had gone to Australia and for many years had worked hard for little pay. Later I had become a riding instructor in Berlin, another low-salaried job. I had given way to the great temptation of living the life of a millionaire in return for furnishing small bits of information to my employer – at least that's how it had appeared to me. Later I was drawn deeper and deeper into the mesh, as was the way with espionage organizations. My actions were to be condemned of course, but could perhaps be understood up to a point. My past, he said with a meaningful look at the bench, was above reproach. I was by no means a professional spy, just an amateur sent on this unsavoury mission by my Israeli masters who were the real criminals and for whom no punishment could be severe enough. He heartily concurred with the prosecution in predicting that the real criminals, the Zionist enemy, would shortly be wiped from the face of the earth. Meanwhile he would respectfully ask the court to impose on me a lesser punishment than the death sentence.

As for Mrs Lotz, that was a different matter altogether. She had not admitted her guilt and she was not guilty. She had trustfully and innocently complied with her husband's wishes, because she loved him. Since when was it a crime for a wife to love her husband? He respectfully begged to disagree with the prosecution's view that Mrs Lotz had been an Israeli agent. There was not a shred of evidence to back up this remarkable statement. And why shouldn't she have met Mr Lotz on a train? In Europe it was not all unusual for a man and a woman to meet casually and get married soon afterwards – a thing fortunately not done in Moslem countries. But European customs were not on trial here. Mrs Lotz was on trial and Mrs Lotz was absolutely innocent of ever wilfully committing any offence against the laws of the United Arab Republic. He moved for acquittal.

That was that. We had had our 80,000 marks worth of defence. Kiesow's lawyers made their plea short and to the point. They presented the court with a dossier-full of newspaper clippings proving that all the factual information contained in his reports to his firm had previously been published in the press all over the world. Therefore there could be no question of divulging secret information. He had been a friend of the Lotz couple. So what! Lotz had had hundreds of friends whom he used for his purposes without their knowledge, and Lotz himself had declared that Kiesow had known nothing of any acts of espionage. If he had made derogatory remarks about the regime, wasn't this supposed to be a free country. If they did not like him, they could expel him from the country but not send him to prison. There was no case to answer, the defence rested.

'The court will pronounce sentence on August the twenty-first at ten o'clock,' announced the president. 'Do any of the accused wish to make a final statement before we adjourn?'

I rose to my feet. 'I do, Your Honour. It concerns my wife. After hearing all the evidence it must be clear to any fair-minded person that my wife is wholly and absolutely innocent of any crime. It is I, and I alone, who am to blame. My wife is perhaps not a very clever woman, but that does not make her a criminal. If, in her innocence and ignorance, she has unwittingly committed any offence against the laws of this country, she has done so under my influence and for my sake. And for this she has already been punished out of all proportion to whatever small wrong she may have done. For the last six months she has been in solitary confinement and she knows she will be separated from her husband for a long time, if not for ever. Let that be punishment enough. I appeal to the court to let my wife free and not to destroy what is left of her life and her youth. As for myself, there is not much I can add to what I have already said. The court knows all the facts and every word I have told was the exact truth. We have had a fair trial and I trust that a fair verdict will be handed down.'

'Thank you, Mr Lotz,' said the president. 'The court is adjourned.'

'That was quite a speech you made,' said Waltraud as the prison van sped back to Kanater. 'What a moving appeal on behalf of your poor innocent wife. Do you think it will help? Anyway, you're a darling and you get A for effort.'

'I don't know if it will help, but we have to keep our image intact.'

'And all the nice things you said about the court, fair trial and so on.'

'Well, five years in Egypt are a great lesson in hypocrisy, darling.'

11

Guilty as Charged

'Entebaa! – Attention the honourable court!' The old court orderly, swelled with the importance of the occasion, ceremoniously threw open the small door which led to the judges' chambers. In all his forty-two years in the courts – first in the Royal Egyptian Courts of King Fouad, later under King Farouk and now in Nasser's United Arab Republic – he could not remember many trials which had drawn such world-wide publicity and lasted so long.

The eyes of everyone in the courtroom focused on him, Rashid el Tantawi, as he announced the imminent entrance of the High Court for State Security, to pronounce sentence in the case of the German spy Lotz, his pretty blonde wife and the other German, Kiesow. This was his great moment, one of the highlights of his career, and Rashid rose to it magnificently. His newly issued white uniform was spotless and his brass buttons, embossed with the Egyptian eagle, shone like gold.

Rashid threw a glance into the judges' chambers. They were just getting ready. It might take another few seconds. Better keep everyone quiet and standing still. He threw out his chest again and with the practice of forty-two years and innumerable trials shouted once more:

'Attention, attention all!'

By now everybody stood, facing the bench. Waltraud and I put out our cigarettes and rose. I looked around. There were about four hundred people all told. Directly opposite us, to the left of the bench, were the reporters, photographers and cameramen – Egyptians, Lebanese, German, French, Americans, among others. Those who had not been able to squeeze into the press enclosure squatted on the floor or stood at the back leaning against the wall. After three weeks of this I had come to know most of them by sight. Some had even managed at one time or other to talk to us for a few minutes. That was forbidden, but the rule was not strictly observed. It wouldn't do to alienate the foreign press. The prosecutor general knew he could trust my discretion and – just to make sure he could – he or one of his assistants always kept within earshot to listen to my stereotype answers. Yes, we were being treated well. No, we had no complaints. Yes, we thought the trial was being conducted in a fair manner.

Some of the reporters who noticed my glance in their direction were nodding at me in a friendly fashion. One fellow in the rear, I think he was French, raised his thumb at us for encouragement. The spectators' benches were crammed to the last square inch. Surrounding the dock sat about thirty men of the Mabahes-el-Amma, the secret police. Stony-faced and watchful they sat all around us, forming a live and effective barrier between the prisoners' dock and the rest of the courtroom. Then there were the university students – at least a hundred of them, brought to watch how justice was meted out to the enemies of their United Arab Republic. They were quiet and disciplined and talked only in whispers.

The German colony in Cairo was well represented. There was the consul – small, dapper, starched to his chin, trying as usual to hide his uncertainty and shyness behind a façade of arrogance and affectation. He was accompanied by his

private secretary, notebook in hand, and a fairly large flock
of embassy and consular officials. Admittedly, they were not
in an enviable position. German-Egyptian relations had
reached breaking-point, and a major espionage trial of German nationals was not helping matters. A little aside from
the others sat young Hiddemann, the German protestant
pastor who had visited us in prison as often as he could,
bringing us books and cigarettes and other small presents.
He smiled at me now as our eyes met and I hoped to God
I didn't look as frightened as he did.

Ten or twelve other Germans were businessmen, repre-
senting German firms, who had come because of Franz
Kiesow. Franz's wife Nadia stood surrounded by Kiesow's
lawyers, trying hard not to show her nervousness.

'Attention!'

That was Rashid's third curtain call and now they
entered, the High Court for State Security of the United
Arab Republic. There were four of them. The three judges
and the prosecutor general who, under Egyptian law, is
also considered a member of the Court. They marched in
single file, heads up, eyes front, heels knocking loudly on
the wooden floor. They were led by His Honour the President of the Court, Hassan El-Badawy. Last in the line was
Samir Nagy, my most intimate enemy.

The judges and prosecutor seated themselves while the
television cameras swept over them. They were dressed in
black suits with a coloured sash across their chest and right
shoulder – the judges' bright green, the prosecutor's red and
green.

The president knocked twice with his gavel.

'The court is in session. Everyone be seated. The court
will now pronounce sentence in the cases of Johann Wolfgang Lotz, Waltraud Clara Martha Lotz and Franz Kiesow.'

I looked at Waltraud. She was pale but seemed quiet and
collected. Leaning across my escort, Major Farid, who had
seated himself between us, I whispered to her in rapid

German: 'Here it comes, darling. Whatever happens, try and be calm, at least until we are out of here. Don't let's give them the satisfaction of a scene.'

Waltraud reached over and pressed my hand. 'Don't worry about me. The luck of the Lotzes will hold.'

'Herr Lotz!' The president was addressing me. I stood up, facing the bench. 'This court has found you guilty as charged. You have been found guilty of continued and re-peated acts of espionage and sabotage on behalf of Israel and directed against the United Arab Republic. The penalty for the crimes you have committed at a time when a state of war exists between the United Arab Republic and Israel is death. However, the court takes into consideration such miti-gating circumstances as were pointed out by your defence counsel and sentences you to life imprisonment with hard labour and a fine of 330,000 Deutschmark. The sentence is subject to confirmation by the president of the re-public.'

A loud murmur went through the courtroom. The spec-tators felt cheated. After all that publicity! Newspapers, television, radio – all had been talking for months about Lotz the German spy, screaming their heads off for vengeance – and now nothing but a life sentence. For me, though, it was a moment of intense relief. I had fully expected to be sen-tenced to death.

'Frau Lotz!' Waltraud rose and clasped my hand under cover of the wooden partition. 'This court has found you not guilty on the charges of espionage and sabotage. You have been pronounced guilty on the lesser charges of aiding and abetting your husband in his criminal activities directed against the United Arab Republic. You are hereby sentenced to three years imprisonment with hard labour and a fine of 10,000 Deutschmark. The sentence is subject to confirma-tion by the president of the republic.'

That was tough. I had hoped so much to get Waltraud off altogether, or at least with a six months nominal sentence already served. But she squeezed my arm confidently and smiled.

"Herr Kiesow!' El-Badawy continued without pausing or raising his eyes. 'After carefully considering all the evidence brought against you, this court has found you not guilty on all charges.'

There were loud cheers from the dozen or so German industrial representatives. The court smiled tolerantly. From the German consul they drew an icy look of disapproval at such behaviour, and that was the last thing I saw. At a sign from my escort, Major Farid, a solid wall of uniformed policemen had formed around us, shutting us off from view. With an apologetic gesture Farid produced a pair of handcuffs, chaining my right wrist to his own left one.

'Let's go. We don't want any demonstrations.'

We were taken in single file down the back stairs to where our transport was parked. A squad of well over a hundred police, rifles at the ready, was formed up with their backs to us and facing a crowd of several thousand curious spectators. All those who had not succeeded in getting into the courtroom now wanted to get at least a glimpse of the German spies.

Stepping from the narrow staircase into the yard I halted, waiting for Waltraud who was coming down behind me.

'Come on, darling, let's give our admiring public their money's worth.'

With a flourish I offered her my left arm – and to cries of 'There they are' and 'Look at the spies' we walked arm in arm to the waiting vehicles, our heads raised high with all the dignity and arrogance we could muster.

12

Tura–Convict 388

Three long and uneventful months had passed since the end of our trial. We were now awaiting confirmation of the sentence by the President of the Republic. This, however, was a pure formality since in all political trials the verdict and the sentences are decided by the President. According to Egyptian law, the President may either confirm the sentence, reduce it or grant partial or full pardon. He cannot increase it. Therefore I was no longer worried about being hanged. Twenty-five years (which is what life imprisonment in fact meant) is, of course, a long time but I never expected for a moment to serve this period. I knew that efforts would be made to get me out and I would also try to escape. Plans for this, however, would have to be postponed for at least three years until my wife was released: if I attempted to escape by myself, the Egyptians might well hold her as a hostage.

While we awaited confirmation of our sentences the privileges we had had after our interrogation and before the show trial still obtained. My wife, who was detained in the women's prison across the road, was still permitted to visit me every morning for one hour – an unheard-of concession. Together we received regular visits from our German lawyer,

Krahl-Urban. Ali Mansour also came now and then. Though he'd been recommended by the German consulate, it had been obvious from the start that he was working hand in glove with the prosecution. Hiddemann, the German protestant pastor, was another of our frequent visitors. A mild, softspoken man, he tried as well as he knew to give us spiritual comfort. The books and cigarettes he brought us, however, were much more to the point. Every month or so the German consul, Dr Geiger, made his appearance. We had first made his acquaintance some time before our arrest. Ramrod-stiff on all occasions and generally ineffective, Dr Geiger was easily the most unpopular man among the German community in Cairo. Meeting us again in prison, he had pretended at first not to have known us before. Blushing and stammering with embarrassment each time he came to see us, he made his visits as short and infrequent as he decently could.

The arrival of the Egyptian newspaper reporters two or three times a week was our greatest diversion. The state-controlled press had been ordered to give an account, embellished with a maximum number of photographs to prove its authenticity, of how well and fairly the German spies were treated in prison. According to the press, these spies, tried publicly and in open court for their crimes, had never been subjected to any kind of pressure or even discomfort – and the good physical condition we were in was visible proof of this! Foreign correspondents received their material directly from the prosecutor's office and were never allowed anywhere near us. With mixed feelings I had read several German publications like *Stern*, *Spiegel* and others, smuggled through to me by one who shall remain nameless. There were extravagant captions like, 'The gay spies in Cairo', or 'The mini-Bond of Israel's secret service'. Another one – on the front page of a small-town daily newspaper in southern Germany – read: 'Their heads are about to roll, while they laugh and jest.' Anything for a sensation.

I shifted and yawned on the bed in my cell. It was impossible to read. Ever since the end of the trial there had been little to relieve the daily routine. The only bright spot was Waltraud's daily visit. That lasted an hour – sometimes longer, if Captain Ahmed Lutfi was in a gracious mood.

For another half-hour I was permitted to walk around in a small enclosed yard, guarded by two armed sentries on the wall and supervised by Sergeant-Major Mohammad Battal, my personal warder. For the rest of the day, all twenty-two-and-a-half hours of it, I was locked in my cell where I had the choice of sleeping, reading – if and when the consul had remembered to bring a few books – or just staring at the walls.

Contact with other prisoners was strictly forbidden and very difficult. Of course, by Egyptian prison standards I was still living in great style. My standard isolation cell, two by three yards, contained all the comforts the prison director could put at my disposal. While all other prisoners had to sleep on the floor with two threadbare blankets and were not allowed any furniture whatsoever, I had a bed, a mattress, a pillow, four new blankets, a small table, a rickety stool and a wash basin in a stand. Then there were the usual two buckets, one for drinking-water, the other to be used as a toilet. Once a day I received – at my own expense – a fairly good meal from the Kursaal restaurant in Cairo. Moreover, I could keep and wear my own clothes. The cleaning up was done by a prisoner under the supervision of Sergeant-Major Battal. I soon learned to watch the sergeant-major like a hawk, for I discovered packets of cigarettes and items of clothing missing after his visits to my cell.

My thoughts were interrupted by a voice calling through the small, heavily barred window, high up on the wall of my cell: 'Ya Hawaga! Hawaga Lotz!' I climbed on to the table and looked out. It was Macky, a prison nabatchy (trusty) working in the office, whom I had befriended. Before the revolution in Egypt Mohammad Macky had been a senior official of the royal customs. Shortly after Nasser came to power, Macky was accused of smuggling a plane-load of gold bars, belonging to the royal family, to Farouk in Italy. He was sentenced to twenty-five years hard labour. He had now served thirteen of them. Macky told me: 'The confirmation of your sentence has just been received in the office. They are transferring you to Tura today. I'm sorry, you're really a convict now, ya habibi!'

'What about my wife?'

'Her sentence has been confirmed too. She'll stay where she is, in the women's prison here in Kanater. Only, now you won't be able to see each other so often. Tura is not a very nice place. But you'll be allright. You have money. You'll be able to arrange things. Listen, ya hawaga: When you get there, give my regards to Victor. He'll help you.'

'Who is Victor?'

'Victor Levy. An Israeli spy. He got twenty-five years. He's been in for about eleven and almost runs Tura prison! Now I must go. That bastard Lutfi is looking for me. Alf essalama!'

With that he disappeared. I got off the table slowly and began pacing up and down the cell. The name of Victor Levy meant a great deal to me of course. I knew he was one of those involved in the Lavon Affair.* I wondered what kind of man he was and if I would ever dare disclose my identity to him. After all he was not only a fellow spy but a fellow Israeli.

Two other men had been imprisoned with Victor Levy, and I'd already learned from my wife that the only woman involved in the Affair, Marcelle Ninio, who'd been sentenced to fifteen years, was in the women's prison. Waltraud had often talked with her and indeed Marcelle Ninio and

---

* The so-called Lavon Affair (named after Pinhas Lavon who was at the time Defence Minister of Israel) took place in 1954 when a spy-ring composed of young Jews and led by two regular Israeli army officers was caught committing acts of sabotage in Egypt.

I had even exchanged notes on several occasions – notes which were written on cigarette paper and hidden in the double bottom of a match box which I had prepared. We had done this before, during, and after the trial.

I turned my thoughts away from Victor Levy, casting them ahead to Tura. I knew there were two prisons which were greatly feared for their strict regime and inhuman conditions: Tura and Abu Zaabal. In the days of the monarchy there had been a special prison for foreigners in Alexandria where conditions were more humane, because it was realized that no European could endure the treatment at the regular prisons for long without serious harm to his health. Nasser's synthetic Arab Socialism had done away with imperialistic privileges like that. Well, there was nothing I could do about it. I might as well get ready for the worst.

Later, as I was about to be transferred, I requested and received permission for Waltraud to visit me for a few moments.

She tried very hard not to show her emotions in front of the Egyptian officer who stood over us. I told her: I'll probably be much better off in Tura. I won't be isolated and I'll have plenty of company. Please try not to worry. It won't be long before we're out.'

But Waltraud was not so optimistic. She pointed out that I had twenty-five years to serve.

'I don't think it will take too long,' I reassured her. 'Two or three years perhaps. The boys will find a way to get us out.'

'You have a lot of faith in them.'

'Yes. They won't let me down. I'm sure of it.'

'Then I'll also try and be sure of it.'

It was time to go. We kissed once – hard – and then she walked out, followed by her guard, her head raised high in defiance and her hands clenched into fists. If I was ever close to breaking point, it was at that moment.

Before leaving Kanater, I was issued with a suit of convict's clothes and ordered to put it on. This consisted of a pair of trousers, a long-sleeved shirt to be worn outside, and a peaked cap. All these garments were made of the cheapest kind of sack cloth and were dyed green. That was all the prisoners wore. Summer and winter, rain or shine. Shoes were not issued. Those prisoners who had their private shoes or slippers were allowed to wear them, otherwise they went barefoot. The clothes I had received were old and threadbare, but at least they were freshly laundered. Everything was about three sizes too small for me. The trousers ended approximately six inches above my ankles. The tiny cap was perched on the back of my head.

When Sergeant-Major Battal appeared, he could hardly suppress a grin at the sight of me. 'What do I look like?' I asked him. He laughed: 'Frightful. But don't let it worry you. In Tura you will get a proper outfit for a few piastres.'

We arrived at Tura prison shortly after five. The prison was situated halfway between the residential suburb of Meadi and the arms and aircraft factories in Helwan, both of which I knew intimately. I had driven on the main road along the Nile countless times, past the heavily guarded stone wall surrounding the prison, with hardly a thought for what might be going on inside the forbidding-looking structure. Now I was about to find out.

The sergeant-major rang the bell at the main gate, and I was led into a wide corridor with office doors on both sides. My handcuffs were removed, and I was told to stand near the wall and wait. Some warders were hanging around, looking me over curiously, but there were no prisoners to be seen at this hour. My arrival was duly registered in a large black diary, and one of the warders was despatched in search of the duty officer. After about twenty minutes two officers arrived, approaching with the exaggerated dignity most Egyptian officers assume. One was a major, the other a captain; both were dressed in well-cut uniforms with shining buttons and badges, carried canes, and wore the standard moustache of the republic. They went into one of the offices, leaving the door open. Seating himself behind a large desk the shorter one, the major, beckoned me. With his cane he pointed at a spot in front of his desk and said in English: 'Stand there!'

This was clearly going to be different from good old Kanater prison. No more 'take a seat, Mr Lotz, have a cigarette, Mr Lotz'. Here it was just 'stand there!' I realized it was imperative to assert myself right away.

'Do you mind if I sit down, major? I'm a little tired,' I said innocently. The captain, who had been sprawling in an armchair, sat up. 'This is prison! Verry strong prisonn!' he shouted in broken English, 'Stand!!' The short major interfered: 'Maalesh,' he said to his colleague in Arabic, 'never mind, let him sit.' He motioned me to a chair: 'Please.' The first round was won. A sergeant-major entered, saluted, and handed the major a large envelope with my papers. He read them through carefully and addressed me again: 'Is your name Johann Wolfgang Lotz?'

'Yes.'

'You have been sentenced to life imprisonment with hard labour. That is twenty-five years according to the law. You are now convict number 388. Remember the number. Your personal belongings will be placed in storage until they can be handed over to your consul. Everything else will be explained to you by the prison director. Perhaps he will let you keep a few personal things. I don't know. It's up to him.'

I took out a packet of cigarettes and a box of matches. 'Do you mind if I smoke, Major?'

'No, no, please go ahead.'

I extended the packet to him: 'A cigarette?'

He glanced at the other officer. 'No, thank you. Not now.' He leaned back in his chair and regarded me: 'Weren't you a friend of General Ghorab?'

'That's right.'

'And of General Abdel Salaam Suleiman?'

'Yes.'

'And of General Fouad Osman, and Admiral Fawzi Abdel Moneim, and many others?'

'Yes, I suppose so.'

With a short laugh he said to the captain in Arabic: 'Da afrit, da. – He is a devil, that one. He knew everybody of importance. In the army, the police, the government, everywhere. And he milked them dry.'

'Yes,' retorted the other angrily, 'and the cream of the milk he sent to Israel! Be careful of that one, Kamal, he is dangerous.'

'Not any more. His dangerous days are over once and for all. Did you know that Youssef Ghorab had been convicted?'

'Yes, I hear he has been dismissed from the police, stripped of his rank and thrown into prison. Now he is at Abu Zaabal. Serves him right!'

I felt genuinely sorry for Ghorab. I had liked the pompous little general with the open palm, always eager to be of service to his rich German friend. What I had done to him was not very nice. But then spies couldn't always afford to be very nice people. Indeed, this was one of the least pleasant aspects of my kind of work. You had to trick and betray people, including some you had come to like, make use of them for your own purposes. But, after all, you had to bear in mind that you were up against an enemy that was developing, among other things, bacteriological warheads that could be aimed at your country.

I was led through various gates into a block in the inner yard. A warder was crouching on the ground half-asleep. On seeing the major he leapt to rigid attention. 'Put this prisoner into an empty cell,' Major Kamal ordered the sleepy warder. 'Search him first.' All of a sudden he slapped the man's face very hard. 'Where are your boots, you son of a dog?' he shouted. Indeed, the warder was barefoot. His

N

boots, I observed, stood on the floor nearby. Hurriedly he
put them on. 'Now button up your tunic, you filthy bit of
rubbish!' the officer continued. 'Report to my office at nine
o'clock in the morning. You're on a charge. Now do your
job!'

The warder hastened to button his tunic – not very effec-
tively, because two of the buttons were missing – and said
to me harshly: 'Get undressed. Take everything off.' I looked
at the major. He nodded: 'Yes, a body search has to be
made. It is the regulation. Get undressed.' I took off all my
clothes which were scanned very carefully. A white civilian
shirt I had been wearing under my prison garb was taken
away. I was allowed to keep my underwear, socks and shoes.
The contents of my pockets – a packet of cigarettes, matches,
a handkerchief and a comb – were returned to me. While I
was dressing again the warder brought two blankets, unlocked one of the other cell doors and threw them inside.

I entered my new home and the door was locked behind
me. Inside it was almost completely dark. There were no
windows, only a very small barred opening in the ceiling.
The cell was about two yards in length and something less
than that in width. The only furnishing consisted of a latrine
bucket in the corner, a water container, a tin cup, and the
two blankets which I now proceeded to unfold. They were
ancient, unbelievably thin and torn in many places. I struck
a match to have a closer look at them. As I had suspected,
they were crawling with lice. I threw them into a corner.
It wasn't going to be a very restful night. I'd known, of
course, that Tura would be rough, but I'd never imagined
anything like this. It was medieval.

Tomorrow, however, I would see what could be done to
improve my living conditions a little. By now I was suffic-
iently acquainted with Egyptian prison management to know
how to bribe the right people and get a few extra privileges
out of them. Unfortunately I didn't have enough cigarettes
– the currency of the prison. First thing in the morning I

would try to get permission to buy more cigarettes as well as other necessities.

It was pitch dark. In Kanater there'd been an electric light in my cell, which I could turn on and off as I wished. Here there were no electric fittings whatsoever. I looked up through the small aperture in the ceiling and saw a piece of sky and two stars. I shivered. The Egyptian night was bitterly cold in November.

After an hour or two of walking up and down the tiny cell, trying to keep warm, I heard a voice calling me out of nowhere in Arabic: 'Ya hawaga! Hawaga Lotz!'

I got up and went over to the door. 'Who is it?' The voice came again: 'Look up. Up here. I'm the soldier on the roof.' Looking up through the aperture in the roof I could see the dark outline of a head. 'M'sa el kheir, effendim – good evening, sir. You are Mr Lotz, aren't you?'

'Yes, I am.'

'I'm to give you regards from Mr Victor. He knows you are here and will try to come and see you tomorrow. I'm to ask you to have a little more patience and he will help you with everything. Here is a packet of cigarettes he sends you. Take care, I'm throwing it down to you.'

'Keep one for yourself.'

'No, no, effendim – Mr Victor has given me plenty. Catch!' A package of Belmont cigarettes landed next to me on the floor. My unseen friend spoke again: 'Look, would you like a nice hot cup of tea? I have made some.' There was nothing in the world I wanted more at that moment – and I told him so. A few seconds later I saw an object being lowered through the aperture. I lit a match and could just make out an old tin suspended from a piece of string coming towards me. It was full of steaming hot tea. I poured it into my water cup and the tin was pulled up again. A loud smacking of lips from the roof made me aware that my benefactor was also drinking.

'Do you know Mr Victor from the outside?' he asked me
after a few seconds.

'No, but we have mutual friends.'

'That accounts for his interest in you. Are you also an
Israeli?'

'Oh no, I'm a German.'

'But you were a spy for Israel, I know that. You are an
enemy of the regime. That's good. Gamal Abdul Nasser is
a cruel and dirty man.'

How typical of Egypt for a prison guard to tell a newly
convicted spy that he considered his president to be a bastard.
No wonder, though. He too, I soon learned, had been in
prison – for deserting from the army – and had received
fifty lashes as well. I asked him how he'd become a
warder.

'I'm not a warder,' he replied. 'We are just soldiers guarding the walls and rooftops of the prison. We're not permitted
to speak to the prisoners. Only to shoot them when they try
to escape.'

'Does that happen very often?'

'Sometimes. If they are caught they're beaten very hard
and kept in the ta'adeeb, the punishment cells, for many
months. That's where you are now.'

So my present quarters were the notorious punishment
cells of Tura prison. I had heard about them in Kanater.
Some prisoners who were taken there never came out again.
Others were crippled for life.

The soldier went on: 'If you're a friend of Mr Victor
you'll be all right. The foreigners always stick together.
And Mr Victor has much influence with the director.'

'What is the director like?'

'Abdallah Amara? He is a dog! He is the son of a hundred
dogs! The son of a dirty mother and sixty-six fathers! You
will meet him. Before him we had Halawany Bey. That one
was all right. He didn't care about what went on in the
prison. Everybody had a good time. He was just interested

in making money. He sold everything he could get his hands on, mostly building materials. He is a rich man now, after four years in Tura.'

The quiet was interrupted by loud and continuous screams from nearby.

'What's that?' I asked the soldier.

'They are beating somebody. It is probably Haany Ghan-naam, the prison adjutant. He likes to come at night and beat the prisoners in the punishment cells – I'd better go back to my post before he sees me here talking to you. Good luck, ya hawaga!'

Somehow the night passed. Early next morning I heard the outer gate open and shut and the warder on night duty being relieved. Volubly he told his relief of my arrival and how he had been slapped and put on a charge for not wearing his boots. I heard other cell doors being opened and prisoners being let out into the yard amidst much noise, shouting and cursing. I knocked on my door. No reaction from anyone. Then I started kicking the door with my shoe, loudly and continuously. After some minutes a voice snapped from the other side. 'What do you want?'

'Who are you?' I asked.

'I am the day warder. What is the matter with you, ya hawaga?'

'I want to wash and go to the lavatory.'

'Ba'adein – later.'

'But I have to go now!'

'Ba'adein.'

I was about to curse him soundly, but controlled myself with an effort, realizing it would get me nowhere. I turned the bucket up and used it for its intended purpose. Then I splashed some of the drinking water on my face, and combed my hair. After half an hour or so my door was opened and a corporal came in. He was small, slender, with blond hair and a moustache. He smiled and shook hands with me. 'Welcome, hawaga! My name is Saadik. Mr Victor sent word to me that he wants you treated properly. Is there anything you need?'

Two prisoners appeared. One of them was a very tall, athletic-looking man, about fifty years old, dark-skinned, with greying hair and a huge grey moustache. He was dressed in blue convict's dress of good material, which was clean and well-ironed and fittted him perfectly. His black shoes were highly polished. The other prisoner was an emaciated old fellow with a thin beard, barefoot, and clad in the torn remains of what had once been a convict's uniform. He was carrying some blankets and a pail of water. Saadik introduced the elegant one: 'This is Fattouh, the trusty of the punishment cells,' he said. 'He'll take care of all your needs while you are here.'

Fattouh greeted me with a wide smile. We shook hands. 'Welcome to Tura, hawaga Lotz,' he said. 'I've heard about you. I'm sorry you had to spend an uncomfortable night, but you arrived late, after the lock-up, so I couldn't do anything for you. It will be different from now on. First of all I have brought you some decent blankets.'

He took the four blankets the other prisoner was carrying and showed them to me. They were brand new and clean. There was also a coconut mat to sleep on.

'Clean the gentleman's cell thoroughly,' Fattouh ordered the ragged prisoner. 'Wash the floor and the walls with water. If I find a speck of dust anywhere I'll break your head. Arrange the mat and the blankets in an orderly manner for the effendi to sleep on. Empty the latrine bucket, wash it and scrub it, and also refill the water container. B'surra – hurry!'

'Khader – at your orders,' the old man replied. 'Please, effendim, may I have a rag to wash the floor with?' 'There are no rags,' came the rough reply, 'use your shirt.'

Then the trusty turned to me, saying: 'Come along, Mr Lotz. Have some breakfast with me in my cell and a quiet little talk.' To corporal Saadik he remarked over his shoulder, in the tone of a superior addressing a subordinate: 'I shall send you some food too.'

Fattouh now led me to a nearby cell, his own. By prison standards it was luxuriously furnished. There was an iron bedstead with a mattress, sheets and blankets, a small round table, two low stools. The floor was completely covered with a thick layer of coconut matting. Some pictures, nudes and landscapes cut from magazines, hung on the walls. He pulled up one of the stools and bade me sit down. From under his mattress he extracted an electric cooking plate, the wires of which he attached to two nails protruding from the wall.

'My private electricity line,' he explained grinning. 'I tapped the main line and led the wire under the floor and through the wall, and then connected it to these nails. That gives me electricity for cooking, and at night I connect a bulb and have electric light.'

'You seem to be doing well for yourself,' I remarked, looking around.

'You'll have the same things soon,' he said, pulling a wooden box from under his bed. 'Which reminds me.' He took from the box a carton of two hundred Belmont cigarettes and gave it to me. 'You'd better have these for current expenses. You can return them to me when you get your canteen voucher. If you want to live more or less decently in this place, you have to pay for everything and bribe everybody. Only don't overpay. Every commodity and every service has its fixed price. To have electricity for cooking and light, for instance, will cost you eighty cigarettes for the installation and another forty every month to the chief electrician, Abu Samia. Every so often an officer will discover the wire and pull it out. That's just bad luck. You wait a couple of days and have it installed again.'

From his magic box he produced some eggs, potatoes, a bottle of oil, a packet of tea and a small bag containing sugar. 'Will eggs and chips be all right for breakfast?'

Over breakfast Fattouh told me that the one meal a day provided by the prison was inedible, and that food could be got in small quantities from the canteen and in larger quantities from outside, via the permitted monthly visit – in my case from the German Consul.

We had finished our meal and were having tea, when Corporal Saadik appeared in the doorway. 'The director is on his way here,' he shouted excitedly, 'I must lock you in now.'

'Go back to your cell,' said Fattouh, quickly stowing away his gear. 'I'll see you later.'

I was duly locked in by the corporal, who was fiddling nervously with his key. My cell shone with cleanliness. The new blankets lay neatly folded in a corner on top of the mat. It must have been at least ten o'clock in the morning, but it was still cold and dark inside the cell. I heard a loud shout of 'Entebaa – attention' and the wooden gate creaking open. An authoritative voice asked: 'Where is the new German prisoner?' 'In here, effendim,' came the reply. A key grated in the lock and my door was thrown open. Before me stood a tall, rather corpulent man, with a dark round face and blond moustache, in the uniform of a full colonel of police. 'Good morning.' He said in English. 'I am the director of this prison. How do you feel?' 'Not very well.' I replied. 'May I know why I have been put into the ta'adeeb – the punishment cells? As far as I'm aware I have committed no offence against prison regulations.'

He laughed. 'Ah, you know about the ta'adeeb already. Didn't take you long to find out. But you are not here for punishment. Every newcomer has to be in isolation for ten days. It's regulations. If I make an exception in your case, other prisoners will complain and I'll get into trouble. You will have to stay ten days. After that you'll be moved to section one where all the other spies are.'

'It's very cold here. Could I have some of my own warm clothes?'

He had my belongings brought in and after examining them closely he gave me permission to keep a warm pullover, some underwear and socks. In fact he gave the impression of a fair and friendly fellow but I was soon to find out that beneath this outward appearance of friendliness he was vicious, corrupt and unpredictable.

He left, and shortly afterwards a warder arrived and announced that I was to be taken to the prison hospital for medical inspection. Escorted by Saadik and the irrepressible Fattouh I walked through several inner gates, each guarded by a warder, until we reached the prison hospital. There was a large stone building and a long narrow bungalow, surrounded by a fair-sized and well-kept garden. About a hundred or more prisoners, in groups of five to ten, were either squatting on the ground or slowly walking up and down. Most of them looked unkempt and dirty, their blue convict clothes in rags. Only a few, who kept themselves apart from the rest, looked clean and comparatively well dressed in blue or white clothes. All were observing me curiously as we entered the hospital grounds. Under a mulberry tree not far from the gate Fattouh called a halt. Turning to the corporal he said:

'Look, Saadik, the doctor is still busy and we have to wait a little. Go and visit your friend, the corporal at the hospital gate. Hawaga Lotz and I will remain here under this tree until you return.'

'What are you talking about!' exclaimed the corporal, 'I was told to hurry and take the hawaga there at once. How do you know the doctor is not free? You haven't been there.'

'Ya Saadik, you son of an ignorant father,' Fattouh retorted impatiently, 'don't you understand the most simple matters? When I tell you the doctor is busy, he's busy! Now, here are two cigarettes, one for you and one for your colleague at the gate. Have a smoke together and come back here in ten minutes. Do I make myself clear?'

The corporal nodded and vanished without a word.

'What was that in aid of?' I asked the grinning Fattouh.

'Somebody wants to speak to you. I'll be back in a little while.'

He walked off and I was approached by a prisoner who had been standing nearby, next to the wall of the main hospital building. This man was obviously not an Egyptian. He was light-skinned and clean shaven, with markedly intelligent features. I guessed his age to be no more than about thirty-five, but his dark hair was already greying.

'My name is Victor Levy,' he introduced himself. We shook hands warmly.

'I'm glad to meet you at last,' I said. 'I can't thank you enough for what you've done.'

He made a deprecating gesture with his hand. 'It's nothing. Unfortunately, I am not able to do much while you're still in the ta'adeeb. I spoke to Fattouh of course and to the warders, and they promised to look after you, but there is very little that can be done to improve conditions in the punishment cells. Once you are transferred to Section One you will have everything you require. I live there too, together with my friends Robert and Phillip, we'll be neighbours. How do you feel now? Is it very bad where you are?'

'Oh, I'll survive, I suppose. I've got some warm blankets now and plenty of cigarettes from Fattouh.'

'Yes, I gave him those for you. When you come to us I shall get you something decent to wear too. In any case you are supposed to wear blue and not green. Blue is the colour of Tura prison. Listen, Lotz: You are going to see the chief medical officer now – Dr Fouad. I just intercepted you en route. Try and get him to put you into hospital for a few days, then you'll be rid of the ta'adeeb once and for all. Failing that, at least ask him to prescribe you a mattress. Tell him you have pains in your back. He is not bad, this Dr

Fouad, but very capricious. I hear you have met the director already.'

'Yes. He seems all right.'

'Be careful of him. He's a bastard. Fortunately I'm on fairly good terms with him.'

'So I've heard. You seem to run this prison.'

'Hardly that. I'm one of the oldtimers here – eleven years – and I know my way around. Now I have to leave you. We don't want to be seen here talking together for too long. They see conspiracies everywhere. We have to be a little careful. You are new here and you are dangerous, so they'll watch you for a while.'

He gave my shoulder a friendly squeeze. 'Don't worry about anything, we'll look after you.'

He gripped my hand and, glancing around to make sure nobody was near, added in an undertone: 'Shalom!'

We walked up to the end of the bungalow. Three steps led up to a spacious verandah, on which four men in dark civilian suits were reclining in armchairs, smoking and drinking coffee. Corporal Saadik made a sign for us to stop at the foot of the stairs. Ceremoniously he saluted the four civilians, who made no acknowledgement of any kind, and marched across the verandah into an office which lay beyond.

'Those are some of the prison doctors,' Fattouh whispered to me, 'it pays to be on good terms with them. Up there is the office of the chief medical officer. If he takes a liking to you all your troubles will be over.'

The corporal was beckoning to me from the doorway. I walked up and stepped into the office. Behind a large desk sat a balding, elderly man sucking an empty cigarette holder. Another, younger man, with a stethoscope round his neck, stood next to him. The one behind the desk addressed me in very good English:

'I am Dr Fouad, the principal medical officer. I take it you're Mr Lotz.' He eyed my bedraggled attire, then shook his head in disgust. 'Are these all the clothes you have?'

'Yes, doctor. Not exactly the latest fashion, and not too warm either.'

'Hm. – You certainly look different from the pictures I saw in the papers.'

'Times change.'

'They do. Now tell me, are you in good health? Is there anything wrong with you?'

'Well, as a matter of fact I don't feel too well. Some time ago I was treated for a gall bladder complaint, and now that I have to sleep on the stone floor I have some pains again.'

'What do you imagine I can do about that?'

'Oh, I don't know. You are the doctor. Perhaps I should go into hospital so I get a bed and mattress to sleep on.'

He turned to the other doctor, speaking in Arabic: 'Dr Sabry, does this fellow understand Arabic?' 'I hardly think so,' came the reply.

Dr Fouad scratched his bald head. 'Actually I wouldn't mind admitting him into hospital for a while. Seems a shame the way he's being treated. But the administration might make trouble again and accuse me of favouritism. You know those buggers. Better make sure first.'

He picked up the telephone on his desk and dialled a number. 'Dr Kamal Assem, please. This is Dr Fouad speaking ... Hello! Dr Kamal Assem? A very good morning to you. How is the family? – That's fine! – Look, doctor, I have here this new German prisoner, you know which one I mean ... Yes, that's right. They're keeping him in the ta'adeeb and he's not so well. I thought perhaps we might admit him to hospital ... What? – Why not? – Hm – Oh yes, I see – Well, in that case ... Yes, of course. Certainly. Thank you, doctor. Ma'assalama!'

He shrugged his shoulders and said to Dr Sabry, still

speaking in Arabic: 'I knew it. This man is regarded as very dangerous and they want him isolated and locked up securely. No admitting him into hospital unless he is very seriously ill. And even then only under special guard and by prior consent of the administration. I don't understand what they're afraid of, but those are the orders.'

He turned to me and said in English: 'I'm sorry, Mr Lotz, we are full up in the hospital. We can only take severe cases.'

He wrote something on a slip of paper and handed it to me. 'Take this. I have presecribed some pills to ease the pain and you can draw a mattress from the stores. That's all I can do for now. And eh.... let me give you a piece of advice: Ask your consul to intervene on your behalf with the prison administration. You might get some extra privileges then.'

I thanked him and went out with Saadik. That was Egypt all over. I knew the pattern: minor officials being afraid of other minor officials – afraid of being suspected of bribery and corruption. Still, at least I had a mattress.

At the stores I received my mattress – a good, clean one – in exchange for fifty cigarettes. Equipped as I now was, I viewed the days ahead with more confidence. At least I would have a fairly comfortable place to sleep and something to eat. The thought that I had some reliable friends in this stinking prison cheered me up quite a bit. I didn't trust the most excellent Fattouh overmuch, useful as he might be, but I was greatly looking forward to having close daily contact with Victor.

Back in the cells Fattouh invited me to inspect the premises. There was not much to see except human misery at its worst. Some of the other cells – no bigger than mine – contained up to fifteen prisoners. Fattouh explained that they took it in turns to sleep. Some squatted on their haunches along the wall while others stretched out and slept. They were locked in most of the time and a truly terrible stench prevailed everywhere. I was made to admire the whipping post, another relic of the middle ages and still an official form of punishment in prison as well as in the army. For lunch (a tasty meal of corned beef and mashed potatoes provided by Fattouh) we were joined by Sergeant Abbas. He was a giant of a man with a big, curled-up moustache and a winning smile. Sergeant Abbas had an interesting sideline: in addition to his regular duties he was also the official hangman. Whenever an execution took place, Abbas had to officiate. Now, sitting with Fattouh and myself and diving deep into the fried corned beef, he winked at me good-humouredly: 'Mr Lotz, I'm very happy I made your acquaintance here over a good lunch and not at the other place. From what I read in the papers I was afraid I would have to string you up one bright and early morning. It would have been a pity. But Allah is merciful.'

He helped himself to another mouthful, smacked his lips, and continued: 'I'm sure you would have behaved yourself and not made a mess like the one we had today. That was a lousy hanging this morning. When I led him out he puked all over me, scared stiff. Well, I gave him one on the ear to remember me by in the hereafter. It's funny,' he mused, 'some behave themselves and some just don't.' With great relish he gave us a detailed account of the numerous hangings at which he'd officiated. Some he'd enjoyed, others not. There was nothing sadistic or bloodthirsty in the way he related his experiences. On the contrary. He seemed a simple and good-natured chap, and he spoke of his work with the pride of a good craftsman.

*　　*　　*

On the morning of the tenth day of my solitary confinement I was told by the duty sergeant to collect my things and move to Section One. Section One, considered a maximum security jail and practically escape-proof, consisted of a huge, forbidding-looking, stone building, four storeys high, with rows of small, heavily barred windows. Surrounded by a massive stone wall with armed guards posted on top of it, it was actually a prison within a prison. A small door, set into the big wooden entrance gate, was opened and we were let into the compound which lay between the wall and the building itself. A warder on duty on the inside of the gate proceeded to search me. At that moment I saw Victor coming towards us with great strides, waving his arm in greeting.

'Never mind that!' he said to the warder, handing him a cigarette. The warder immediately stopped searching me, smiled, and motioned us in.

'I've been waiting for you,' Victor said to me. 'Let's go up. You'll be on the fourth floor where all the so-called "dangerous political prisoners" are. It's supposed to be the strictest section of the whole prison, but actually it's the cleanest and most comfortable. We live there too. Your room is ready.'

Having reached the fourth floor we were received by a stoutish, dark-skinned warder. Victor introduced us: 'This is Abu Khris, the sergeant in charge of our floor. He does not give us any trouble.' Then he ordered the sergeant: 'Open the room for the hawaga.' Getting into the spirit of things I offered Abu Khris a cigarette, which he accepted with dignity. He then produced an immense iron key and opened one of the cells. 'Come in,' Victor said, 'how do you like it?'

I stood flabbergasted. The cell itself was the standard two by three affair with one small barred window. But this cell had been transformed into something which, under prevailing conditions, was nothing less than a palace. The walls had been freshly painted in light blue. On the floor beneath the window a thick, brand-new mattress was spread out covered with equally new blankets, a pillow and some sheets. Other blankets were used as floor-covering. There was a folding

table and chair, a small cupboard and even a bookshelf with
some English books on it. An electric light bulb hung from
the ceiling. The latrine bucket, scrubbed to a bright gleam,
had a wooden toilet seat fastened to it, and in a corner,
attached to the wall, was a water container with a tap. Even
a picture, a landscape painted in oils, hung on the wall.

'That is a welcoming present from Robert, the third of
the three musketeers,' Victor explained when he saw me
looking at it. 'He is quite a painter.'

'Victor, I really don't know what to say,' I exclaimed.
'I'm rather overwhelmed by all this unexpected luxury. How
did you manage it?'

He laughed. 'I have my connections. I'm glad you like it.
Better try and be as comfortable as possible, you may be
here for quite a few years yet.'

'It's funny how you learn to appreciate the little comforts
of life when you're in prison,' I replied. 'A year ago I
wouldn't have considered it possible even to exist in a place
like this, and here I am happy as anything over a clean
prison cell and a few pieces of primitive furniture.'

'Here, let me show you something,' Victor said. He
reached out and removed the bottom part of the bookshelf.
It was hollow and contained an electric cooking plate, a
knife and a packet of coffee. 'All useful, forbidden little
items,' he smiled. 'For the time being, until you get properly
organized, you'd better have your meals with us, but you
may want to make some coffee at night or have something
to eat.'

A prisoner entered, carrying two cups of steaming coffee.

'This,' said Victor, 'is Mohammad. He will be your nabatchy, your personal servant.'

This was the most incredible thing of all. I was to live
like a lord with a servant – in Egypt's deadliest prison. But
I was soon to learn that the prisoners with money all had
their own personal servant to clean their rooms, to wash
their clothes, to prepare their food and to smuggle for them.

For this they were paid between five and six cigarettes a day. Victor explained to me that, as everywhere in Egypt, there was a great difference between what is and what should be. This fourth floor was for dangerous political prisoners. Here the prisoners had all been sentenced to hard labour, but in fact few of them did any work at all. It was considered safer to keep them isolated and away from the original prisoners whom they might corrupt politically.

Victor related how ten years ago he and his other Israeli friends had been made to work in the quarries about three miles from the prison. They had worked there for three years. It had been back-breaking work, with hardly any food and plenty of beatings. He went on to explain that every new arrival was defined as prisoner Class Three for three years. After he'd served the three years in the quarries he became prisoner Class Two, which meant that he worked in one of the workshops inside the prison compound. After six years the prisoner was up-graded to Class One where he didn't have to work at all or could choose the work he wanted to do. This up-grading also entailed other privileges such as extra letters, a little primitive furniture, and more canteen money.

Class One prisoners had 10 Egyptian pounds per month, Class Two £7 and Class Three £5. But few prisoners had money at the office and £10 was a fortune to most of them. Ten pounds was, in fact, the monthly salary of a sergeant-major with twenty-five years seniority and a large family. Victor reassured me that I wouldn't have to manage on £5 per month. He'd heard in the office that at the request of my German lawyer I'd been placed into Class One right away. The same applied to my wife. As regards letters, he promised me that I could write to my wife as often as I wanted. This he did through the good offices of Major Kamal who very much liked American cigarettes and Swiss chocolate.

Alone in my solitary cell, I had wondered how I would

o

manage to pass the time but again Victor reassured me on
this point. 'According to the regulations,' he said, 'political
prisoners should be locked in their cells for twenty-three
hours each day, but this rule is seldom fully enforced.'

The cells were opened at about seven in the morning,
then locked again for two hours at midday and finally locked
at around five in the evening. During the opening hours one
could do more or less as one liked within the section. Actually, political prisoners were not permitted to speak to anyone or to visit anyone in their cells. This rule was also not
enforced. The prison authorities turned a blind eye to such
particulars, not out of the kindness of their hearts but simply
because it would have been too much trouble to enforce
rules of this kind.

I asked Victor how he'd managed to live like this for
eleven years and he told me that only the first three years
had been really rough, when he and his friends had been
beaten frequently. This was because they represented the
worst combination of all – that of being spies and Jews into
the bargain.

'You're lucky being a German,' he said, 'that saved you
from a few unpleasant experiences.'

'Like hanging for instance?'

'Yes, you were a big fish. But as you're a German, Nasser
preferred to let you live for political reasons. The economic
situation is disastrous and is getting worse all the time. He
needs all the support he can get – and now he hopes to get
more from Germany.'

'I wonder how long he'll stay in power?'

'The prisons are full of people who plotted against him
and failed. Some of them are your neighbours here on this
floor. Let's go down into the yard. I'll introduce you around.'

We went down the iron stairs into the yard. Scores of
prisoners were walking up and down singly or in small
groups. In a corner, some distance away from the others,
stood a group of six or seven men, who, to judge from

their dress and general appearance, obviously belonged to the upper classes. We crossed the yard to join them.

'Gentlemen,' Victor said, 'meet Mr Lotz, the latest addition to our community.'

They all turned to greet me in the most cordial manner, and, shaking hands all round, they were introduced to me one by one.

'Mr Abdul Rahman Salim, espionage for CIA, ten years.

'Mr Karam Ismail, espionage for CIA, fifteen years.

'Mr Said Lutfi, political sedition, twenty-five years.

'Dr Ezzeddin Abdel Kader, political sedition, twenty-five years.

'Captain Ahmed Lutfi, formerly of the Egyptian Navy, espionage for British Intelligence, twenty-five years. His father was hanged for the same offence.

'Mr Riad Osman, espionage for CIA, twenty-five years.

'Mr Kamal Abdul Razzak, political sedition and espionage, fifteen years.'

'Well, gentlemen,' I said, 'I seem to be in good company.'

13
Rate of Exchange

It was spring 1967, and I'd been in prison for two years. During this period I'd spent a great deal of time with Victor Levy and the two other convicted Israeli spies – Robert Dassa and Philip Nathanson. By now the three had learned of my real identity, and in a rather amusing way. Previously they had known me, of course, as a German who had spied for their country, and on this basis they had helped me – often at considerable inconvenience and danger to themselves. As a result we had become close friends and I often spent many hours with them in their cell where they talked about Israel and their experiences there.

Although they used to converse in French among themselves, my own French was poor, so conversations in my presence were always held in English. One day, about three months after my arrival in Tura, during a discussion on Israeli politics, Victor and I happened to disagree. We argued for a while until Robert, thinking that I would not understand, said in Hebrew to Victor: 'You can't expect this gentile German to understand the finer points of Israeli politics.' I could stand it no longer, and laughing loudly and speaking Hebrew I said: 'You schmock, I'm as much an Israeli as you are.' After that, Major Ze'ev Gur-Arieh (my Hebrew name) of the Israeli intelligence became, of course, a full member of the club.

The separation from Waltraud was more appalling than I had expected it to be and even the considerable privileges Victor won for me did little to compensate for her absence. The German Consul was useless except for supplying monthly parcels of food and cigarettes. I repeatedly lost my temper with him. I smoked like a chimney – and ended up in hospital with a heart attack. Hospitalization was a comparatively pleasant interlude, yet it only served to make me realize that the sentence hanging over me was interminable and that the conditions of the less 'privileged' prisoners around me were appalling. Now I could understand what the Jews had been through in Egypt – and indeed what dissenting Egyptians had been through too. So much for Nasser's socialistic policies!

After a few months I had partially recovered, though I still remained in hospital. It was at this stage that I became involved with Victor, Robert and Philip in a somewhat hare-brained plan to tunnel our way out of Tura.

Victor and Philip had access to the outer yard, and the plan was to dig a tunnel from the inside of a tool shed (situated next to the outer wall) to a point outside as far away as possible from the watchtower. When the tunnel was finished, Victor and Philip would smuggle Robert and myself into the shed under some pretext, and we would then, all four of us, try to make our escape. This could be done only during the day, and among other things it meant adapting our prison uniforms to resemble civilian clothes. And then what? It would be vital to have outside help if we were to stand any chance – to have a safe hiding place, forged passports, proper clothes, good make-up.

One of our number, Robert Dassa, had already served fourteen of his fifteen year sentence and we considered it only right that he should serve out his sentence – just one more year – and not be involved in a dangerous scheme

which had, at best, a fifty-fifty chance of success. After some
reflection, though, he insisted on joining us, which showed
the kind of man he was. As it turned out, however, external
events were to take us by storm and override our plans.

Daily, it was becoming clearer, from what we read in the
Egyptian newspapers and heard from officers, that the public
was being systematically prepared for war. Anti-Israel and
anti-Western sentiments were artificially brought to fever
pitch at mass rallies and by the press. These feelings were
reflected by many of the prisoners and my own position
became somewhat delicate. I was a German, the native of a
country with which the United Arab Republic had broken
off diplomatic relations because of its pro-Israel stand, and
a spy into the bargain. Searches of my belongings became
more fequent and supervision more strict; prisoners and
guards with whom I had been on fairly friendly terms were
all of a sudden afraid to be seen talking to me. This tense
atmosphere reached its climax when radio and newspapers
announced that the Egyptian navy had closed the Straits of
Tiran. Egypt's number one journalist and Nasser-intimate,
Mohammad Hassanein Heykel, boasted in his leading article
that this action was meant to provoke Israel into attacking
the UAR – whereupon the Egyptian eagle would pounce on
the Jewish chicken and tear it to shreds. Apparently the
liberation of Palestine was at hand. Coloured posters showing a caricature of a Jew being crushed to death by the
boot of an Egyptian soldier and Uncle Sam being kicked
in the behind by the same boot were put all over the prison
compound. The radio blared out an uninterrupted pro-
programme of martial music and speeches full of blood and
glory. It seemed as though war would break out any moment.

One day Victor brought the news that all political
prisoners would soon be discharged from hospital and sent
back to the cells. Orders to that effect had been received
from the prison administration who wanted the politicals
isolated. Standing orders directed that in case of air bom-

bardment in the immediate vicinity of any prison the gates should be opened and the prisoners let out – all except the politicals, who were to be shot. Nice prospect.

The next morning I was called to the chief medical officer.

'It has been decided to discharge you from hospital,' he told me, 'you will go back to Section One.'

'Do you consider me cured, Doctor?' I asked innocently.

'Well, you are much better than you were.'

'A little better perhaps, but surely not cured. What will happen if I have a heart attack at night in my cell with nobody around to give me an injection or call a doctor?'

'I can't help that, we have our orders. You will still be under hospital conditions. We will give you a bed and mattress and a medical attendant will be stationed in Section One. If any of the political prisoners needs a doctor, he'll call one. It won't be for long. The war, once it starts, will be over in a few days and you'll come back here. If you need something, come and see me any time.'

There was no point in arguing, he couldn't change the orders. I was ordered to pack my belongings and move to Section One.

The next morning, June 4, the air raid sirens began to sound. It was around eight-thirty and most of the political prisoners were taking exercise in the yard of Section One.

I looked out of my window which commanded a fairly good view of the area beyond the outer prison wall to the north, north-east and north-west. Everything seemed to be normal. Cars and trucks were driving along the Cairo-Helwan road, barges were sailing up and down the Nile, and a train was letting off passengers at Tura station. In accordance with standing orders for air-raid alarms, no prisoners were to be seen inside the compound, and the armed guards on the walls were trebled. I took my cooker from its hiding place, made myself a cup of coffee, and began to read. Suddenly there was loud and persistent knocking on the wall joining my cell to that of the next door prisoner, Abdul

Rahman. I got up and went back to the window. Our barred,
paneless windows were set close together, so that we could
speak to each other without raising our voices. Often at
night, when sleep evaded us, we would stand there and talk
for hours.

'What is it?' I asked him. 'Is the war starting or something?'

'Believe it or not, it is!' he cried excitedly. 'Didn't you
hear the explosions?'

'What explosions? I heard nothing.'

'I'm not joking, Rusty, there were three or four heavy
explosions. Stay near the window, perhaps you'll hear some
too.'

There were several loud detonations in close succession.

All of a sudden the martial music, which had been continuously blazing from the loudspeaker, stopped. 'We are
interrupting our programme for an important announcement,' an excited voice was saying. 'War planes of the Zionist enemy, reinforced by American bombers, have attacked a
limited number of targets near the capital. Only minor
damage was sustained and most of the cowardly attackers
were shot down by the gallant pilots of the United Arab
Republic. Our beloved leader, President Gamal Abdul
Nasser, has immediately ordered the complete occupation
of all Palestine. Already our armed forces have penetrated
deep into the territory of the so-called State of Israel,
which will cease to exist in a very few days. A Holy War
has been declared and the sword of Islam unsheathed. Further communiqués will follow at hourly intervals though-
out the day. A military band will now play the national
anthem.'

The next communiqué was broadcast an hour later: 'Armoured divisions of the United Arab Republic are advancing
rapidly into Israel territory and have already occupied many
towns and villages. Some of the vehicles at the head of the
conquering columns are equipped with loudspeakers through
which orders are being given to the Jewish population to

clear the streets and remain in their houses. Palestinian Arabs, who for years have been forced to live under the Zionist yoke, are extending an enthusiastic welcome to our heroic troops. They are dancing in the streets, many of them weeping with joy and relief. Large concentrations of Israeli troops and armour are completely encircled and in the process of being destroyed. Over eighty Israeli warplanes were shot down in the first two hours of the war and they keep falling from the skies like dry leaves from a dead tree. Tomorrow – if Allah the Merciful wills it – our heroic soldiers will perform their evening prayers in Tel-Aviv.'

In the late afternoon we were let out of our cells for half an hour. I tried to see Victor and was told by one of the guards that all the Jewish prisoners had been taken to the punishment cells 'for their own protection'. We were then made to stand by in front of our cells to await an announcement by the prison director. After a few minutes the director's hoarse voice came to us over the public address system:

'Officers, soldiers, prisoners – my brothers! This is a great day in the history of the Egyptian people. A great day in the glorious history of our republic and of the Arab nation. The enemy has declared war on us and we have taken up the challenge. Large parts of Palestine have already been conquered by our victorious army and it won't be long before the last Jew is driven from the Arab homeland. Rejoice, my brothers, as I know you will! Today it makes no difference whether one is an officer, a warder or a prisoner. An Egyptian heart beats in our breast and we all share the same feeling of national pride. Our country is in a state of war and this places a great responsibility on all of us. Each and every one of us must do his share to achieve a quick and final victory. I expect all prisoners who are given a clean bill of health by the doctors to donate blood for our soldiers in the front line. The number of working hours in the quarries and in the workshops will be increased. At the

same time the prison staff will be reduced, because officers
and guards are needed to run our prisoner-of-war camps.
Many thousands of Israeli prisoners-of-war have been captured, among them over three hundred of their pilots. Owing
to this temporary shortage of warders in our prison, you
will not receive any visits until the present emergency is
over. There will also be a complete blackout at night throughout the prison.'

Immediately he'd finished, we were all locked in again.
Pacing up and down my tiny cell between door and window
I tried to appraise the situation from what little I'd heard.
Past experience had taught me to mistrust the bombastic
announcements of the Egyptian news services and it was
obvious that all their blood-and-glory speeches and so-called
news items could not be accepted at their face value. On
the other hand, there had to be at least a grain of truth in
them. If only ten per cent of what they claimed was true,
then Israel was in a grim position indeed. But how could this
have happened? It just didn't make sense. The Israeli Army
could not have been taken by surprise. It was unthinkable
that they had not been aware of the huge military build-up
in Sinai. I thought it far more likely that they had known
the exact disposition and location of the Egyptian forces.
I remembered the thoroughness with which my own reports
had always been examined and discussed. No detail was
too insignificant to be taken into consideration, no rumour
too vague not to be followed up and verified. There was no
reason to assume that the present set-up was any different.

How much truth could there be, then, in the triumphantly
proclaimed Egyptian victories? Their war potential couldn't
have improved to that extent since my arrest. The Egyptian
Army, as I remembered it, had been in no position to wage
a modern war, let alone win it. No quantity of Russian
arms and equipment could change that. As long as the
Egyptian way of doing things – in other words, the Egyptian
mentality – remained what it had been for centuries, they

would continue to be children who played at being grown-ups, much to the chagrin of the foreign experts and instructors they employed.

But could their boasts of having occupied large parts of Israel and having shot down scores of aircraft be entirely baseless? Hard to say. The 'penetration deep into Palestine' might easily boil down to the occupation of one or two Arab villages. Some aircraft might also have been lost, although the bombing of targets near Cairo, which the Egyptians admitted, did not make it likely that a critical situation existed on the Israeli border, hundreds of miles away.

However, all this was pure speculation. In a day or two some true facts would perhaps emerge. I missed Victor's tiny transistor radio – hidden in a tin of jam – which I often borrowed to listen to the news from Israel, the BBC and the Voice of America. But Victor and the other two boys were in the ta'adeeb and I had no way of knowing what happened to that precious tin of jam.

All I could do was wait, which was harder than ever under the circumstances. It was pitch dark inside the cell. The lights had not been turned on because of the blackout and without a light I could not try to pass the time in the usual manner by reading or writing a letter to Waltraud. I was wondering in what way the war might affect us personally. The possibility of a decisive Egyptian victory was too remote to be considered seriously. A stalemate perhaps, which would hardly change our situation. And what if Israel won the war? She would be in a position to dictate terms to the UAR. They might even get them to release Waltraud and myself. It was hard to believe this. Nevertheless, all the time my hopes were increasing. But what if the Egyptians carried out their plan to shoot all political prisoners in case the war came too close to home?

That night we heard Israeli planes bombing somewhere in the vicinity of the prison, presumably at the military war factory in Helwan. It gave me a certain amount of satisfaction to realize that some of these targets had been pin-pointed by me. I only hoped the planes were not going to drop any of their load on *my* head by mistake. The bombing went on for some time and in the general black-out I could see explosions from my window. About half an hour later I heard footsteps outside. The key grated in the lock and my cell door was thrown open to reveal Lieutenant-Colonel Youssef Timras, accompanied by four or five warders. He was furious and shouted at me to get out of my cell.

'Haven't you done us enough harm already,' he screamed at me. 'One of the sentries on the wall has reported that you set fire to a newspaper and waved it out of your window in order to guide Israeli aircraft.'

I couldn't convince him that this would have been a silly and ineffective thing to do, and that it must have been flashes from the explosions that the sentry had seen. I was chained and led at gun point to one of the punishment cells. The next day all the other political prisoners were transferred to the solitary confinement block.

Gradually we realized that the war was not going so well for the Egyptians – and later still we discovered that it had been disastrous. One morning Abdul Rahman came in with the incredible news of Nasser's resignation. Later the radio was turned on again and, walking through the yard towards our fellow prisoner Mustapha Amin's cell, we heard the news bulletin. It said that the president had indeed announced his intention to resign and that parliament would convene that afternoon to make a decision on the matter. Meanwhile, the announcer said, American bombers, supporting the Israeli airforce, were constantly attacking Egyptian positions. UAR troops were fighting heroic battles and had inflicted heavy losses on the Imperialist-Zionist enemy. Several Israeli divisions had been wiped out and the towns of Khan-Younis and El-Arish retaken by an Egyptian task force. Lines of defence had been shortened in a few places for tactical reasons. The Suez Canal was closed. The United Nations had asked for a cease-fire. The Soviet Union had condemned the imperialist aggression in the strongest terms and threatened to interfere actively on the side of the UAR. Traitors and Zionist agents were spreading defeatist rumours, which the public was not to believe. A temporary setback did not constitute a defeat and the great Arab nation would yet emerge victorious. 'Peace and the blessings of Allah be upon you,' the bulletin ended.

The others had also come out of their cells to hear the news and we were all standing together in a group.

'What do you think of Nasser's resignation?' I asked Mustapha Amin.

'A bluff. So far he has announced only his intention to resign and has put it up before his gang of yes-men in parliament. He only wants them to beg him to remain in office. I bet you anything you like that at this moment they are organizing demonstrations asking him to withdraw his resignation. "We want our beloved leader, the saviour of the nation." You know how it's done. They bring in a few hundred truckloads of villagers and factory workers, pay them five piastres each, and make them run through the streets shouting "long live Gamal Abdul Nasser". Then he will bow to the will of the people.'

We little realized at the time how exactly history would bear out Mustapha's prediction – and in only a few days' time!

A loud call of 'Attention!' was heard from the outer yard, a sign that an officer was approaching, perhaps the director. A guard shooed us quickly into our cells. A few minutes later Major Kamal came into my cell, closing the door behind him. All the political prisoners rather liked the little man who was always polite and well mannered and often went out of his way to grant privileges not provided for in the regulations. He could be depended on to be blind and deaf at the proper time and his prices were reasonable.

'How are you, hawaga?' he said, shaking hands with me and seating himself on the bed. 'Mind if I sit down? I heard they'd put you all in solitary. What a silly thing to do! I just wanted to see how you were getting on.'

I asked him if he had any news. He replied:

'The news is so contradictory, one doesn't know what to believe. None of it is good. I meant to ask you something, hawaga – you are our military expert here.'

'I am?'

'Well, yes. With all your war experience in the German army you know much more about military tactics than any of us here. We are just police officers.'

'But I know very little of what is going on, only what the news bulletins say.'

'You will be able to tell me this. What does "second line of defence" mean? It's a military term, isn't it?'

'Yes. It means exactly what it says. When a military formation has to retreat in the face of an attack, in other words to give up its foremost defence positions, it withdraws to a second line of defence at some distance behind the first.'

'How far is that?'

'Oh, that depends on a number of things. The topographical structure of the terrain, for one. Sometimes there is a rear line of fortifications or else the commander will choose the kind of terrain that can most easily be defended. A mountain chain, a river, anything that presents a natural obstacle to an advancing enemy. Why do you want to know all this Kamal? Do you intend joining the army?'

'Not I, I am too much of a family man. Hawaga, you have explained this very nicely, but I don't understand half of what you say. All I want to know is this: the military commentator announced that our fighting divisions in Sinai have withdrawn to the second line of defence. Where exactly is

that? How far have the Jews advanced? Can you explain
that to me in a few simple words?'

'How should I know that, Kamal? I hear the news on the
radio, same as you do, that's all.'

'I hear a lot of rumours too and everybody says something else. El-Arish is gone, Sharm el-Sheikh is gone, the
Mitla Pass is gone, what have we still got? Next thing we'll
be hearing is that the Jews are in Meadi. Where is this
second line of defence they're talking about?'

'The Suez Canal would seem the most likely choice.'

'Will that stop them?'

'Your guess is as good as mine.'

'It's a terrible situation. Terrible! It's unbelievable! Why
did he have to make war? Why didn't he stay at home and
mind his own business? What's wrong with peace?'

The door opened and Abdul Rahman looked in.

'Oh, I didn't know you had a visitor. Good morning,
Major Kamal.'

'Come in and sit down,' I invited him. 'Major Kamal and
I are discussing the war.'

'I have some news,' he said, sitting down on the bed with
us. 'One of the guards has a brother in the army who
managed to escape from Sinai and got home last night. He
says there is nothing left of the Egyptian army. They are
either dead or running for their lives. The Israelis have
crossed the Canal and General Dayan has established his
field headquarters in Fayid. They are advancing on Cairo
without meeting any opposition. It is said that Nasser and
Field Marshal Amer have escaped to Yugoslavia with their
families.'

'Is this true?' said Kamal, his face the colour of chalk. 'If
the Jews get here they will slaughter everybody. The
officers first. Or they will turn the prisoners loose on us and
they will cut us to pieces.'

'Don't be a child, Kamal, and don't believe such nonsense,' I said. 'I'm quite sure all these rumours are vastly

exaggerated. It stands to reason. It is possible that the Israelis
have occupied both sides of the Canal, but they won't ad-
vance into Cairo unless they are complete fools, which obviously they are not.'

'What's to prevent them?' Abdul Rahman wanted to know.

'Their common sense, that's what. Even assuming they
could occupy Cairo without a shot being fired, do you realize
what it takes to administrate a city of this size? Over three
million people live here, more than the whole population of
Israel, not counting the area between here and the Canal with
towns like Suez and Ismailia. Let's say four to five millions
altogether. Estimate what that means in terms of food, medical and sanitary services, police and everything else that
comes under the heading of administration, even temporary
administration. I think we can discard this possibility entirely,
it's just not feasible.'

But to me anything to do with Israel suddenly seemed
feasible. I felt an immense pride.

We remained in the punishment cells for twenty-one days,
locked in most of the time. The war was over, but the
prison authorities took their time about turning on the electric light again. Spending the best part of the day in semi-
darkness, which made reading impossible, and the nights in
complete blackout, each day seemed an eternity. Kamal's
DDT did not help much and my body was covered with
bug bites. The itching only increased my irritation. Food
was scarce. I was always hungry and lost a great deal of
weight. The only commodity we did not lack was news.
Many of the officers and guards visited us daily and actually
seemed eager to tell us all they had seen and heard outside,
and to discuss it with us. Many of the second- or third-hand
reports were grossly exaggerated, like the one putting the
number of Egyptian casualties at 200,000 soldiers killed in
Sinai alone; but altogether we received a pretty clear
picture of what was going on in Egypt itself. Nasser and his
secret police were ruling the country with an iron fist, nip-

ping manifestations of discontent in the bud by arresting
anyone who was even suspected of expressing criticism of
any sort. Even so, they did not entirely succeed in prevent-
ing the people from giving vent to their feeling in various
ways.

The initial shock felt after the total defeat at the hands
of the Israelis was followed by a general feeling of disgust
and anger. The fairy tale about the American bombers had
quietly been dropped and was explained away as a 'misunderstanding'. To the last man, woman and street urchin the
population was well aware that it was Israel alone who had
administered the defeat. Army officers were afraid to show
themselves alone in public places. Even our own prison
officers, who were members of the police force, avoided
wearing uniform in the streets. Each morning they came in
civilian clothes and changed into uniform in their offices.
This practice was adopted after an incident in which a
uniformed officer had stopped a taxi to take him home.
The driver had stuck his head out of the window and spat
on the ground saying: 'If you could run away in Sinai, you
can walk now.'

'Look at this,' Mustapha Amin said to me one morning,
pointing at a page of *Al-Ahram*, the daily newspaper he
received regularly and read to us aloud during the short
period we were allowed in the yard. 'They're even forbid-
ding the jokes now.' There was an article on the front page
admonishing the public not to tell anecdotes detrimental to
the régime and likely to undermine morale. Offenders would
be punished.

We'd in fact heard an incredible eyewitness report from
a warder about an incident in the village of Mansouria, not
far from my farm. Police had come to arrest a man who had
made derogatory remarks about the government, and some
of the villagers had forcibly prevented the police from taking
him away. An hour later the village was surrounded by a
large police detachment, supported by armoured cars. A

P

portable aroussa, or whipping post, was erected in the village square and all male inhabitants given a severe lashing. Those considered to be ringleaders were taken away and not heard of again.

Our transfer back to the fourth floor was followed by an announcement from the prison director to the effect that as from now prison routine would return to normal. Weeks and months went by. Twice or three times a week I wrote to Waltraud and also received letters from her more or less regularly. They were reassuring letters, telling me she was well and in good health and hoping that the war would bring about our early release. She too was short of food and other commodities, but I was not to worry, she could manage for a little longer on what she still had, until the consul awoke from his lethargy. We were both trying hard to cheer each other up and display a degree of optimism we did not always feel.

Radio and daily newspapers were full of reports of how well the Arabs had the situation in hand. The Arabs were holding summit conferences, sub-summit conferences, economic conferences and press conferences. The UAR was getting financial aid and had the material and moral support of nearly all the world. Soon the brutal aggressor would be brought to his knees. A new, bigger and better army was being built up and revenge would be taken. No Israeli ship would ever pass through the Suez Canal and what had been taken by force of arms could only be regained by force of arms.

Another newspaper report stated that Field-Marshal Amer had committed suicide and that there was no truth in the rumour that he had been murdered at the president's orders: there were the copies and photostats of any number – in fact, of far too great a number – of medical reports to prove that. Large headlines announced the arrest of Salah Nasr, the chief of intelligence, and his top aides, among them our friend Hassan Aleesh. They were the ones largely to be blamed for the defeat – the 'set-back', was the official term for the deb-acle. They had falsified intelligence reports, used public funds for their own private purposes, and even tortured innocent citizens.

One morning in early November I was called to the Ad-jutant's office. There I met Krahl-Urban. Immediately he told me: 'I have very good news for you, Wolfgang. I told you about the efforts that are being made all the time to secure your release. Gigantic efforts, I can tell you! Until recently the Egyptians refused point blank even to discuss it, but now they have agreed in principle to release you and that should be quite soon.'

All I could fumble out was, 'When you talk about me, that includes Waltraud of course?'

'Oh yes, but your wife is no problem. Her sentence is almost up. It appears that you'll be released on medical grounds and deported to Germany.'

'The main thing is to get out of this damn country.'

'You will, you can count on it.'

'And what about Victor and the others?'

'I'm not too sure but as far I know they should also be released.'

Returning to Section One I immediately relayed the good news to my three Israeli friends. In a few weeks at most we would be out. Victor remained sceptical. 'I hope you are right,' he said. 'Every so often we hear rumours about a release, a pardon, an amnesty – after fourteen years of this I can't quite bring myself to believe it any more.'

'But this is not a rumour, Victor. This is virtually a certainty!'

'We shall see. I hope so.'

I looked up and saw the expression on his face And I spent the rest of the day cursing myself for my lack of sensitivity.

Over the next days I could detect a marked change in the attitude shown to me by my captors. Suddenly I seemed

important to them – and they seemed less sure of themselves
when they approached me. But nothing happened and I
began to have some doubts. Christmas Day 1967 arrived,
and with it Waltraud's visit. The allotted time for our visit
was two hours and it took place in the office of the deputy
director, Youssef Timraz. Waltraud was clad in the simple
white dress of the women prisoners, but to me she looked
more beautiful than ever. She had let her hair grow and she
looked younger than I had remembered. She came into my
arms and for a moment we were silent. Youssef Timraz and
Lieutenant-Colonel Mohammad Subhy, the director of the
women's prison, who had accompanied her, turned away.

Waltraud and I sat down together on the sofa and talked
in German, telling each other of our experiences in prison,
both minimizing the hardships we had to endure and touch-
ing mainly upon the lighter side of prison life, poking fun
at the Egyptian methods of running things. Soon, however,
we turned to the subject foremost in our minds – our release.

I tried to be as optimistic as possible and I told Waltraud
that I had the utmost confidence in Krahl-Urban and never
doubted for a moment what he had told me.

Three weeks later, on January 14, 1968, I was called to
the prison hospital where Victor and Philip were already
waiting outside the principal medical officer's room. They
told me excitedly that we were to come up before a medical board which would recommend our release on medical
grounds. Robert, they said, would be released on other
grounds because fourteen of his fifteen years' sentence had
already been served.

I was the first to be called into the office. Behind a table
sat Dr Kamal Assem, chief medical officer of the prison's
administration department, and two other doctors I did not
know. They asked me only my name – and then, without
even a formal examination, they proceeded to write out a
medical report stating that I had terminal cancer and a very

serious cardiac complaint, that my maximum life expectancy was three months and that my release on medical grounds was recommended. I was then discharged.

I waited outside until Victor and Philip had gone through the same comedy. When they emerged, the three of us – cancer and cardiac patients – were taken to the office of the director. Abdallah Amara beamed at us and said that he already had our release papers on file but that it would be another few days before instructions came through for our actual departure. A few days turned out to be another three weeks and naturally we all became more than a little tense. Finally, on February 3, 1968, I was called to the adjutant's office.

When I entered, the adjutant rose from behind his desk and stepped forward to greet me with outstretched hands.

'Awalan mabrouk!' he said with a wide, insincere smile. 'First of all – congratulations! You are free! You will leave for Germany tonight.'

'You are free.' How many times in the last three years had I paced my cell or lain on my bed imagining those very three words. I had pictured myself either jumping up and down with joy or sinking into a chair, feeling faint with relief. Now that the great moment had actually arrived, my most fervent wish fulfilled – I felt nothing. It was an anti-climax. I was surprised at being so unmoved, at not being able to summon up the kind of emotion appropriate to such a moment – but there it was.

'Thank you, captain,' I answered politely. 'That's very good news. What's the procedure now?' My voice was normal – almost flat.

'You will go to the paymaster's office and collect your money and then you will change into your own clothes. They are in the empty office next door. You can go and take anything else you want from your cell, and then you'll be escorted to the airport. I'm glad to see you go, you have been a lot of trouble to us.'

'Well, your troubles are over now, and so are mine I hope. Am I the only one to be released?'

'Your wife, too, of course.'

'What about the other boys?'

He shrugged: 'They are on the release list, but . . .'

After receiving what money I still had to my credit at the paymaster's office I proceeded to put on my civilian clothes, the few garments that had not been stolen by Ali Mansour, who was supposed to have taken charge of them. There were three suits and half a dozen shirts which – three cheers for the consulate – were freshly laundered and ironed. Victor, who was always the first to receive prison news of any kind, was there to help me re-pack my suitcase and see me properly dressed. Then we went back to Section One to collect a few small items I did not want to leave behind, but mainly to say goodbye to some of my fellow prisoners.

For the last time I walked through the walled-in yard. I met Mustapha Amin, who had come to shake my hand and wish me luck. 'You must write a book,' he said. 'Let the world know what the inside of Egyptian prisons looks like.'

We shook hands once more and I turned to go. Hassan El-Hodeiby, head of the Moslem brotherhood, was sitting on a stone bench. Shaking and heaving, the old man got to his feet when he saw me. 'Let me wish you luck, Mr Lotz,' he said with feeling, 'I am happy for you, you are a good man. May God bless and protect you.' He placed his shaking hand on my shoulder and kissed me on the cheek. I had not expected so much emotion from this quarter.

'Where are the others?' I asked him. 'I want to say goodbye to them too.'

'They were here a little while ago,' he replied, 'I think they went back to their cells when they heard you were leaving.' He smiled apologetically. 'Do not be angry with them, Mr Lotz, they have all been here in prison a long time. It is perhaps natural that they should be envious you are being released after only three years.'

I took my leave of Robert and Philip, who were not permitted to leave their cell block, and accompanied by Victor I went to the director's office; he nearly took my arm off shaking hands with me and wishing me all the luck in the world. Then I had to take leave of Victor. My escorts – three police majors – were already waiting and impatient. Victor had been told by the director that his release would take another few days. I hoped fervently he would not be disappointed again, as he and the others had been after the Sinai Campaign in 1956, when they had harboured great hopes of being released and been bitterly disappointed when their expectations failed to materialize.

Victor kept straightening my tie and buttoning my jacket, until we finally embraced with some emotion and parted. I was handcuffed and taken in the back of a police lorry to the passport office at the Ministry of Interior, in the centre of Cairo: there I met Waltraud.

'We've made it!' I exclaimed, throwing my arms around her.

A few moments later Dr Bartels, the new German consul, made an appearance. He seemed relieved that there had been no last minute hitch in the arrangements for our departure. His short stay in the country had already taught him that last minute hitches were the rule rather than the exception when dealing with Egyptian authorities. He handed us a sum of money and told us that we'd get our tickets and passports from the police at the airport.

'I will come and see you off in the morning,' he said.

'In the morning? But we are leaving at four this afternoon.'

'Who told you that? Your flight leaves at three thirty tomorrow morning.'

'Then we'll have to wait another fifteen hours.'

'They'll take you to the airport now and you can wait

in the transit lounge. I dare say it's more comfortable than the place where you've been waiting the last three years.'

'In that case I'll have to get these chains off,' I said. I beckoned to one of the police officers. 'Look here, we shall have to wait for many hours yet, and I want you to remove my handcuffs. I'll give you a pound each.'

He deliberated for a while and then went into conference with his two colleagues and another police officer who had escorted Waltraud.

'Take them off,' counselled Waltraud's guardian. 'What are you afraid of? Do you think he'll escape?'

'All right,' said the one who seemed to be in charge of the expedition, 'one pound now and another pound at the airport. For each of us.'

'Agreed.'

He unlocked the handcuffs and put them in his pocket. In return I handed over three one-pound notes.

At Cairo airport, I handed over the other pound notes as we moved into the reception hall. Our four officers saluted when a man in civilian clothes approached us. Secret Police was written all over him.

'You can go,' he said. Then he turned to us. 'Good afternoon, I shall remain with you until you take off. Please follow me.'

At a nod from him customs and passport control officials stepped aside to let us through without the usual formalities. He led us into the transit lounge.

'I won't bother you,' he said. 'I'll sit here near the entrance and you may move around in the lounge or in the restaurant upstairs as you wish. Please don't talk to any of the other passengers. It is in your own interest to make your departure as quiet and inconspicuous as possible!'

Hamdy, Samir Nagy's assistant then appeared, all bows and smiles. After expressing his happiness at our release, he explained that Samir himself was tied up in court and sent his apologies – he would very much have liked to come himself to say goodbye. Hamdy returned to us several personal items that had been in Samir's care and which he wanted to return as a token of 'friendship and affection'. They included my fountain-pen, my wallet, Waltraud's movie camera and – incredibly – nine *undeveloped* rolls of cine film. Later, when I gave the films to Israeli Intelligence they were flabbergasted to think that no one had thought of developing them: 'We see it,' they said, 'but we can't believe it.'

* * *

Our Lufthansa plane, coming from Karachi, touched down soon after midnight. The consul had come to ensure our safe departure and sat with us making small talk. Then he suddenly told us, in a hushed voice, the true extent of the amazing negotiation that had surrounded our release. As I listened I could hardly believe what he was saying – but nevertheless he assured me that it was all true. Following the Six Day War the Israeli Government had refused to return 5,000 Egyptian prisoners of war (including nine generals) until ten Israelis languishing in Egypt's prisons were released! Two of these were Waltraud and myself. I was astounded. Here I was being swopped – and the Egyptian authorities must have fully realized, for some weeks now, my true identity. And yet, to save his own face, Nasser and the heads of his Intelligence had been forced to maintain an elaborate and ironic pretext, even up to the very last moment.

Accompanied by the consul, our guard, an air hostess and a police officer in uniform, Waltraud and I walked over to the aircraft. The police officer handed us our passports and stood aside, watching us enter the plane. He took no chances and remained standing there until the door was closed.

'Fasten your seatbelts please.' The engines came to life and we taxied across the tarmac to the end of the runway.

'Here we go,' I said to Waltraud. But we didn't. The noise

of the engines died down and an announcement came over
the public address system.

'Ladies and gentlemen, may we ask you to be patient for
a little while. The control tower of Cairo airport has not
yet given us clearance to take off. Our departure may be
delayed. Thank you.'

What had happened? Were we not going to be released
after all? Had the Egyptians changed their minds?

We looked at each other, neither of us daring to express
the dread we were beginning to feel.

'This is a German airliner,' Waltraud was saying. 'Are
we technically on German territory – or can they still take
us off?'

'No, no, this is German territory.' I lied as convincingly
as I could. I looked out of the window. There was a fire
engine some distance away, but no police.

'What's holding us up?' I asked the air hostess.

'Some small formality. We'll take off in a minute.'

'Yes,' I thought. 'You'll take off. But without the Lotz's.'

It turned out to be a twenty minute wait. It was the
longest twenty minutes I have ever known. Then, suddenly,
with a slight jerk the aircraft began to move forward,
gained speed on the runway and finally rose into the air.
Waltraud held on to my hand.

'I feel sick,' she said.

'Relax, everything will be all right now,' I said, looking
down as Egypt disappeared. 'All our worries are over,
darling, once and for all.'

'Yes, now we can really start thinking about the future.
What are we going to do?'

'First we'll take a nice long rest, have a holiday – and after
that we'll decide what to do. The main thing is that we're
together again.'

'You know, it reminds me of that letter you wrote to me
just before our trial when you said, "the happy Lotz's will
ride again".'

'The happy Lotz's will indeed ride again – but this time in Israel.'

'Remember all those plans we made, Wolfgang, about finding a house in the country and settling down to a quiet life. Were you really serious?'

'Ah, Lotz the country squire. Yes, I was serious.'

'Well now that I know you mean it, I can really relax. I was half expecting you to tell me what our next assignment was going to be!'

Epilogue

Four years have passed since our release from prison. My wife and I have settled in Israel, in a village outside Tel-Aviv. Waltraud has aquired Israeli citizenship and learned to speak the language of the country fairly fluently. I have now retired from the army and work with a large private firm of investigators, dealing among other things with bank and industrial security. We have realized our dream of a house in the country, and live there with our four dogs. Although we lead a happy, comfortable and quiet life, it often seems an anticlimax after the hectic and adventurous years in Egypt.

When I got back to Israel I was shown some of the practical results of my work in Egypt, in the form of photographs and other documents. These gave me the satisfaction of knowing that in my own way I had made a small contribution to the successes of the Six Day War. I often show my friends the nine undeveloped cine films the prosecutor general was kind enough to return to me.

Naturally the experiences we went through left their mark on us in many ways, especially the years in prison. When we were designing our house, for instance, we both insisted on having very large rooms because small rooms reminded us too much of the prison cell. For many months after moving in I used to get up in the middle of the night and walk out into the garden – just to savour the wonderful feeling of freedom and to confirm that I could actually open a door at will, go wherever I pleased.

Waltraud remains good looking, full of energy and has retained her irrepressible sense of humour; but her health has suffered somewhat, mainly as a result of the brutal methods of interrogation and the years in prison. I have put on a bit of weight and sometimes find myself short of breath when I ride too hard: riding, incidentally, remains one of our passions. As far as our social life is concerned Waltraud has made one condition with which I heartily concur – that we invite to our home only people we genuinely like. If occasionally I have to see or entertain someone for purely business reasons, I do so elsewhere. The hospitality of our home is strictly for our friends.

The three Israelis who were in Tura prison with me all live in Tel-Aviv, are married and have children. Victor Levy is an agricultural engineer, Robert Dassa is studying Oriental Sciences and Philip Nathanson has become a photographer. Marcelle Ninio, who was released shortly after us, married recently and Prime Minister Golda Meir gave the bride away. The five of us get together frequently.

It is a little harder to keep track of all the others who in some way or other played a part in our Egyptian venture. Franz Kiesow still works for the German firm of Mannesmann abroad. Gerhard Bauch disappeared completely for a while and even the most persistent newspaper reporters were unable to discover his whereabouts. He is now said to be with the German Embassy in Washington. Our Dutch friend, Hank Wenckebach, who had been Director General of Shell in Cairo and retired some years ago, recently visited us in Israel, staying with us for a couple of weeks. In Cairo of course he had known me as a former Nazi and this had been the one flaw in our friendship, for as a Dutchman he

had no love of Nazis. In Israel he recalled how one day at
the Cavalry Club, when we were having coffee with some
Egyptians, I absent-mindedly drew a swastika in the sand
with my riding crop. When he remarked that he didn't care
very much for that particular symbol I had replied flip-
pantly that those, after all, had been the great and glorious
days. He became furious, stalked out of the club, and didn't
return for ten days.

Waltraud's parents had rather a hard time of it. Her father
is a diabetic and also suffers from a heart and lung ailment.
So the three weeks he and his wife spent under arrest in
Cairo didn't improve his condition. The Egyptian intelligence treated him well by their standards but he still had
to undergo an operation after his release. When my parents-
in-law returned to their home town of Heilbronn, in
Southern Germany, they were pestered incessantly by newspaper reporters and virtually had to barricade themselves in
their flat. Whenever they looked out of the window, they
were at once photographed from the street. One newspaper
reporter slid a signed blank cheque under their door with a
note saying: 'We want an interview. You fill in the amount.'
Another sent them a note saying: 'Five thousand marks for
five minutes interview.' In fact, when they were released
from prison I had asked them specifically not to give any
interviews of any kind to the newspapers – and they never
did.

Shortly after Waltraud and I returned to Israel they both
came over to see us. As I waited for them at the airport, I
confess to having some misgivings as to how my father-in-
law would react. After all, I had married his only and much-
beloved daughter, had carried her off to Egypt of all places,
made a spy of her and finally landed her – and them – in
prison. However, when they arrived their only concern was
whether we were in good health and whether there was
anything they could do for us. To this day I have never
heard one word of blame or reproach from either of them.

Of the Egyptians I knew in Cairo, most were arrested,
interrogated for weeks and later released. Some of the officers
I had been friendly with were cashiered, others were allowed
to retire from the army. It was established, of course, that
they had taken no active part in my espionage activities,
but the authorities considered that they had been careless in
their talk and in their relationships with foreigners; furthermore, they had also accepted a great number of valuable
presents which the authorities regarded as bribes for services
rendered or favours granted. All this was disclosed during
my interrogation and even then the prosecutor-general,
Samir Nagy, had declared angrily, 'I shall stamp out this
vermin.'

Poor old Youssef Ghorab got the worst of it, I'm afraid.
He was stripped of his ranks, dishonourably discharged
from the police force, thrown into prison for over a year
without trial and deprived of his pension. He has now
returned to his native township of Damanhur in the Nile
Delta, where he owns a small house.

Johann Von Leers died of old age soon after I left Egypt.
Dr Eisele, who had been a narcotics addict for years, finally
despatched himself into the next world with an overdose of
morphine – a far easier death than the one he inflicted on
many thousands of concentration camp inmates.

The German experts have all left Egypt now and have
been replaced by Russians. In 1964 the exodus of the German
experts had already started in earnest. Some were afraid of
the Israelis, others left because they were thoroughly disgusted with the Egyptian administration. A little later, when
the Russians took over in force, both the aircraft production and the rocket building programmes were abandoned,
and the last remaining German experts dismissed by their
Egyptian employers. Today the aircraft factories in Helwan
serve as assembly plants for Russian MiG planes. Whatever
rockets the Egyptians have are all of Russian manufacture
and are supplied by them.

Waltraud and I are often asked about our feelings towards the Egyptians in the light of our experiences, and people are usually astonished to hear that we harbour no hatred whatsoever for the Egyptians, who very wrongly consider Israel their arch enemy and have been at war with us for twenty-four years. The part allotted to me for several years was that of fighting the war of espionage, the silent battle behind the scenes. It was often hard and not always pleasant but it was a job that someone had to do.

Waltraud and I, like most Israelis, would much rather have Egypt for a friendly neighbour. We want very much to visit Cairo again one day – this time as genuine tourists.